Real, practical insi

VP Distri

This book is an invaluable guide for everyone interested in improving communication. The book becomes a checklist to make certain none of the essential steps is ignored. I plan on using the 5 Strategies in the launch of a new product department. Redmond is right on target.

~Pat Leishman, MBA

A practical approach to current workplace issues and solutions, entwined with a healthy dose of ethics, respect, and civility.

~ Katherine Penny, Director, School of Hospitality and Tourism Management, Ryerson University.

Too often we forget and take for granted the basics and benefits of communication. Something so simple yet dangerous to the organization if it's not done properly. Kathleen really takes a back to the basics approach to this book that made it easy to apply in the real world at our workplace. It really made a difference to all of our employees at every level!

~ Colin Moore, Regional Director of Operations, YUM! Restaurants Canada

Kathleen has worked with our managers and they are benefiting from the concepts. This book summarizes the components of effective communication in an easy to apply manner.

~ Janet McMillan, Community Services of Newmarket and Aurora

Rules of Engagement for Communicating at Work

Rules of Engagement for Communicating at Work

5 Strategies for Decreasing Conflict and Increasing Collaboration

by

Kathleen Redmond

Engagement Publishing
2004 Toronto, Canada

Kathleen Redmond & Associates
1111 Davis Drive, Unit 1, Suite 174, Newmarket, Ontario, L3Y 7V1
Tel. 905.478.7962 Fax 905.478.7945
kr@kathleenredmond.com • kathleenredmond.com

Second Edition, 2005
Published by Engagement Publishing, an imprint of Kathleen Redmond &
Associates

National Library of Canada Cataloguing in Publication
　　　Redmond, Kathleen, 1952-
　　　Rules of engagement for communicating at work : 5 strategies for
　　　decreasing conflict and increasing collaboration / by Kathleen Redmond.

　　　Includes bibliographical references.
　　　ISBN 0-9734038-1-0
　　　1. Communication in management. I. Title.
　　　HD30.3.R42 2004　　　658.4'5　　　C2004-901705-5

Edited by Christine Tomaselli
CommuniCritters Cartoons by Patricia Storms
Cover and text design by Karen Petherick
Graphic Art by Stew Wallace
Cover photo Gerry Images

Printed in Canada

Disclaimer: Names have been changed to protect confidentiality.

DEDICATED TO

Terry James Russell, my beloved husband,
for his patience, understanding, unfailing encouragement
and humorous approach to life's challenges.

ACKNOWLEDGEMENTS

The gestation period for this book was long and challenging. I would like to offer my sincere appreciation to the people who helped this book find the light of day.

... Keith Postill and his organization, for generously sharing their insights and experience.

... Elizabeth Beveridge for her creative ideas, research and way with words.

... Christine Tomaselli for her razor-sharp, precise and elegant editing style.

... Stew Wallace for transforming my ideas into graphics and models.

... Karen Petherick for her intuitive grasp in bringing the book together.

... Patricia Storms for bringing the CommuniCritters to life.

... Susan Clark and Lisa Martynuik for their administrative support.

... Brian McCartney, Peter Webb, Adrian Davis, Pat Leishman, Janet McMillan, John Walker, Wayne McCulloch, Janice Smith, Valerie Dixon and Jody Eagen for the rich and helpful feedback. What a great reminder that we all view the world differently.

... I'm grateful to the advisors who have helped me on my journey to find solid, applicable tools, models and resources. Josef Rich, MSW, and Peggy Grall, a seasoned and practical psychotherapist and long time Employee Assistance Counselor, were extremely helpful in this regard. Ann Armstrong, PhD, Rotman School of Business, University of Toronto, and Julia Christen Hughes, PhD, University of Guelph were generous in the book review and feedback process.

... Special note of thanks to Betty Stirling and Robert Armstrong for their support and encouragement.

... People of the workplace, for all the precious glimpses, challenges and stories that ignited a life long search for solutions.

CONTENTS

Strategy Five – Harness Conflict

Leading Your Team

FOREWORD

I'm convinced that everyone wants to succeed in the workplace. We want to do the right thing. However, there are times when we aren't sure what the "right thing" is, or when we do know, we encounter obstacles that derail our positive intentions. Good people with good intentions often leave organizations when they become unclear about their role and their value in the workplace.

Why is it so challenging for people to communicate successfully in the workplace? Organizations are comprised of individuals with different communication styles, needs and expectations. And it's because of these differences that people continually struggle to communicate in an effective manner.

Communication refers to the way we talk, how we listen, how we behave, what we think and what we believe. It allows us to articulate our sense of reason. It's a gift and an art that requires skills and practice in order to realize its full potential.

During a career that has spanned 25 years, working as an employee and manager in unionized and non-unionized organizations, a management lecturer in university and college programs as well as a corporate trainer and coach, I've come to the conclusion that better communication is tantamount to better business. Time and again, I've witnessed how improved communication positively affects workplace relationships, productivity, morale and employee retention.

This book includes concepts that have been helpful to many people, and I thank the researchers and authors who have created a rich bank of information and ideas to include and build upon. It's my sincere hope that you find the *Rules of Engagement for Communicating at Work* helpful to you as well.

Kathleen Redmond
Sharon, Ontario

INTRODUCTION

Character is at the Heart of Communication

Every word was polished and presented with clarity, careful emphasis and strong eye contact. He nodded discreetly when other people spoke and then reiterated the point that he was there to make. He was flawless, effortless and focused. After he left the room the participants turned to each other and said, "He's moving up rapidly in this organization and I wouldn't trust him with a ten foot pole. The only person we believe is Sam. He's earned our trust."

The days of style without substance are over.
Your people want more, they want the real thing!

Traditionally, training has focused on only one aspect of the individual - the outer most rung of our character - our "communication skills." The experience of working with scores of people in college and university classrooms, corporate workshops, meetings and coaching sessions has taught me that it engages the total person - our entire character - to communicate effectively. Our character has several layers, some more obvious than others, but our words and actions result from the interplay between these layers.

The Layers of Character –
A Communication Perspective

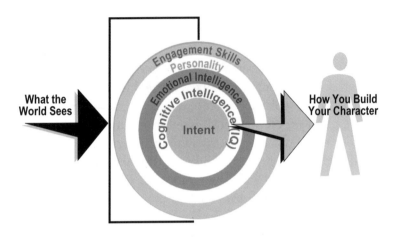

Non-shaded layers represent aspects of your character that are relatively fixed. Shaded layers are yours to manage.

INTENT
Beliefs ... **what you believe about communication, other people and yourself as defined in your communication principles, values, rights and responsibilities**

- *principles* – what you believe as true and important
- *values* – your guidelines regarding how to treat yourself and others
- *rights and responsibilities* – the balance between your responsibilities and the responsibilities of your organization

Goals ... **your communication priorities, objectives and standards**

- *priorities* – vary at different points in time and situations - what's most urgent, second most urgent and so on
- *objectives* – what you're trying to achieve at a given point in time, in one conversation or interaction
- *standards* – the quality, quantity and/or level of excellence in a situation
  More about INTENT in Strategy One and Strategy Two.

Cognitive Intelligence (IQ)

- a person's reasoning abilities, IQ is measured by problem solving tests
- poor predictor of success
  More about IQ in Strategy Two

EI - Emotional Intelligence

- the ability to manage your own behavior by acknowledging and adjusting to your emotional reaction at any given point in time

- the ability to recognize an emotional reaction in another person and adjust your interaction to produce the best end result
  More about EI in Strategy Two

PERSONALITY

- your natural gifts, temperament, talents, preferences and styles
  More about PERSONALITY in Strategy Two

ENGAGEMENT SKILLS

- the skills you employ to communicate with others
- what you say, the words and body language you use to say it

  More about ENGAGEMENT SKILLS in Strategy Three, Four, Five

This is a good example of how character can affect your communication style:

> Pauline was an enthusiastic and engaged participant in the Communication Skills workshop. She eagerly soaked in the information, had many good answers and was given feedback, complimenting her ability to deal with a thorny situation in the small group exercise. At the conclusion of the workshop, as Pauline headed back to her office, she was stopped by George, a coworker and a participant in the workshop. George was anxious to discuss a problem about a late shipment leaving the office. He was clearly irritated and frustrated. His approach toward Pauline was aggressive and he blamed her for not providing him with enough information. Right then and there, in the well traveled hallway leading to the meeting rooms and cafeteria, Pauline lost it, "George, I sure as hell did tell you about that hold up and sent three updates to you as well! Do you ever read your damn email? It's always someone else's fault, never yours. Grow up and take some responsibility!" George's anger clearly escalated and Pauline stomped back to her office. The order never got shipped because George and Pauline's problem never got resolved. Consequently, serious damage was done to both the customer and to George and Pauline's working relationship.

What went awry? Ironically, Pauline had just left a workshop which focused on improving communication skills. Well, communicating appropriately and consistently isn't that simple. It takes more than knowledge and a little practice. It takes all of you - your intent and ability to manage your actions and reactions and your skill - in every interaction. Pauline's character was demonstrated in several ways. Let's analyze what was actually revealed.

First of all, let's look at INTENT. Pauline's *communication principle* regarding how to treat a person was that it was acceptable to strike back immediately and without thought when she felt attacked. Her *communication value* in this situation allowed this conversation to be held in a public place in front of coworkers and without preparation. It was her *communication right* to defend herself and attack George. She didn't identify any *communication responsibilities* for herself. Her *communication priority* was to, "just do it and move on." Her *communication objective* was to attack, blame and humiliate George.

Next, let's look at the EMOTIONAL INTELLIGENCE aspect of this conversation. George was obviously upset. Pauline overlooked this fact. Pauline was irritated by the affront and she ignored her own warning signals.

Finally, let's take a look at the ENGAGEMENT SKILLS used or not used. This was a problem solving moment. Pauline and George's words were blurted out without thought or structure. No problem was solved – the situation was made worse.

Ok, now let's flip this around….same scenario.

Pauline is confronted in the hall by George who asks her about the late shipment. Pauline assesses the situation and says, "George, it looks like you've had a tough day trying to meet the deadline. Let's walk back to the office and figure out our next steps." George agrees and they walk back together. To lighten the situation, Pauline makes a comment about rush hour at the office, saying, "This place looks like a train station at 6:00 p.m.." They both chuckle a bit and George agrees. Back at the office they sit down and work through the problem to find a short term solution. A couple of days later, Pauline asks George to meet with her and talk about the confrontation in the hall. They have a constructive, honest conversation and develop a plan to alleviate any other shipments going out late and to ensure that their conversations have positive results. The process of confronting and solving problems has reaped increased mutual respect and collaboration.

So, what was different in the second scenario?

A lot was different. Let's look at this in stages. INTENT – Pauline's *communication principle* was to treat George with dignity, no matter what. Her *communication values* illustrated that the discussion required a private, calm environment to talk it out. Her *communication priority* was to defuse the situation as quickly as possible and to develop a solution. Her *communication objective* was to work with George to find out what was happening and to get the order shipped.

Her EMOTIONAL INTELLIGENCE told her two things. First, George was in a highly emotional state and a quick, logical discussion was not going to take place, so she used empathy and a bit of humor to calm the situation. She also felt her pulse quicken and knew that she needed to breathe and buy some time for herself in order to think rationally. When they both sat down back at the office Pauline used ENGAGEMENT SKILLS to hold a productive, solution focused conversation. When the urgency of the moment passed, she further confronted the inappropriate behavior in the hall, explaining her perspective and listening to George so that they could agree upon a course of action.

The scenario between Pauline and George demonstrates the layers of character required to consistently communicate appropriately. In order to reach a positive outcome, Pauline needed to clarify her *communication beliefs* so that she could determine her *communication goals* quickly and logically. She possessed an understanding of the power of emotion, in herself and others, that allowed her to adjust her approach. She understood and practiced effective ENGAGEMENT SKILLS so that her words and actions were appropriate and aligned to her communication intent. This scenario illustrates that the way in which we interact with people at work, and with people outside the office, relates directly to the way in which we have developed our *character*.

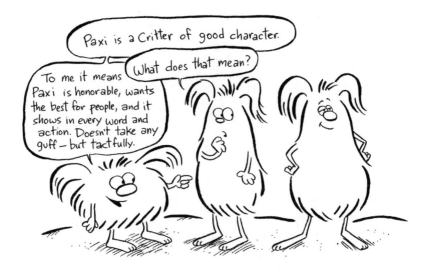

Character and the Five Strategies

The Five Strategies; Clarify the Culture, Know Your Character, Respect Yourself, Respect Others and Harness Conflict are interdependent, and brought to life by you, through the layers of your character. The effective interplay of all aspects defines the *Rules of Engagement for Communicating at Work.*

Clarify the Culture – the systems, processes and protocols that provide the "what," the content of workplace communication

Know Your Character – description of the layers of character and what "you" bring to work

Respect Myself – how to keep yourself balanced and effective while working with others

Respect Others – the knowledge and skills for working with others

Harness Conflict – managing conflict at work in order to derive the benefits and minimize negative aspects

Rules of Engagement for Communicating at Work

LET ME EXPLAIN ...

The CommuniCritters

The Critters are imaginary, genderless, raceless beings brought to life by the talented cartoonist, Patricia Storms. They explain salient points with humor and a sense of fun. The Critters also appear in the learning materials that accompany this book. Several are present on a regular basis. Paxi is a Critter who has worked hard to develop good character and who enjoys the dynamic give and take of the workplace. Migi is constantly out of control, and Nye won't take responsibility for anything, ever.

The two Critters at the water cooler are *snide* and *nasty* in their comments. You see them in a much more positive frame of mind when they help conclude each Strategy.

AND THEY CALL IT COMMUNICATION....

From the Redmond Journal
These are notes from my journal, compiled over an eleven-year period, with the focus exclusively on workplace communication. The notes represent stories, observations, questions and snippets of conversations.

Reality Bites
These are short excerpts from the journal. Sometimes they're the words from the workplace and sometimes they are my observations and comments.

Origin of the Concepts
My quest to learn more about communication and working with adults took me back to school in my 30s to complete a master's degree in Adult Education. My education is ongoing, and no doubt will carry on for the rest of my life. The concepts included in the book are derived from several sources which include:

- compiling research from various disciplines including psychology, leadership concepts, organizational development and the neurosciences,
- studying and receiving certification in programs and training systems including mediation training, emotional intelligence training, Myers-Briggs Type Indicator™ certification, Master Trainer certification with Development Dimensions International, and
- corporate coach training, an international program conducted through Corporate Coach University.

I've outlined the concepts that have proved most helpful in improving communication in the workplace. The majority of the concepts are the work of gifted researchers and authors, who are referenced throughout the book.

The Character Model started to germinate when I noticed resistance to learning about communication. I often heard a remarks like, "This is who I am and I have no intention of changing – take me or leave me." Looking at communication within the context of layers of character decreases apprehension that the person will somehow be "less than themselves" as well as focuses the learning within a particular context area.

The Five Strategies have developed over the years as I've worked with groups and individuals through the rewards and roadblocks of implementation and measurement of their outcomes.

Summary of Key Thoughts and Putting it into Practise
There's a summary page at the end of each Strategy, identifying the key thoughts for each section and ideas for implementation.

Leadership Component
The final chapter is comprised of implementation suggestions for leaders, Strategy by Strategy.

Troubleshooting
This includes a list of workplace communication questions and the Strategy and section that responds to that particular issue.

References and Acknowledgements
References are listed at the back of the book, by Strategy, to indicate the author of a particular concept or piece of work.

STRATEGY ONE
Clarify the Culture

COMMUNICATE YOUR WAY TO SUCCESS

"How well we communicate is determined not by how well we say things, but by how well we are understood."
～❧～

Andy S. Grove, Chair, Intel Corporation

Introduction

Communication. It's a beautiful thing when it's done well, but can have disastrous consequences when it's done poorly. It takes the brunt for all the things that go wrong in an organization, but rarely is lauded when things go right. It's a mysterious phenomenon, indeed. The term "communication" is defined in this book as the way that people interact with each other at work.

From the Redmond Journal

Do you give your heart, soul and first priority to your job? Do you work weekends to meet deadlines? Do you sometimes miss events with your kids because you need to work late? Do you get the recognition you deserve because of your obvious dedication?

If the answer to the last question is "no" – then you're not alone. It amazes me how many people give their "all" to their jobs, but are so undervalued by their employers. No wonder employees get so easily discouraged. It's a significant reason why companies lose great talent. There are so many ways to prevent employee turnover, and it all begins with communication.

Over the Water Cooler

"The left hand doesn't know what the right hand is doing around here."

"Even if I did speak up, who would listen?"

"I've said time and time again, it needs to change. I'm done talking about it."

"The only time I hear from anybody is when something goes wrong."

"Meetings, meetings... what a waste of time. Everybody just smiles and nods and nothing is really accomplished."

Communicate Your Way to Success

Communication refers to the way we talk, how we listen, how we behave, what we think and what we believe. It makes us superior to other species on earth because it allows us to articulate our sense of reason. It's a gift and an art, one that requires skill, practice, and intelligence in order to realize its full potential.

This book will show you that communication doesn't have to be such a challenge, that the barriers blocking communication don't have to be your barriers and that you can enjoy a rewarding and fulfilling work experience by developing your own effective communication style.

Let's get started by taking a look at the organization.

The Importance of Communication in the Workplace

Communication is the lifeblood of the workplace. It creates and maintains the culture of our organizations.

Education and technical skill once stood high atop the list of criteria used by employers to predict the future success of an employee, and therefore, the criteria used to make hiring decisions. Times have changed, and so have those criteria.

According to a 1989 survey conducted by the U.S. Department of Labor, the skills employers were looking for in entry-level workers, after ability to learn on the job and technical skills, were:

1. listening and oral communication,
2. adaptability and creative responses to setbacks and obstacles,
3. personal management, confidence, motivation to work toward goals, and
4. group and interpersonal effectiveness, cooperativeness and teamwork skills at negotiating disagreements.

You can see that two of the four criteria were purely communication skill-based, and the other two had strong communication components. By 1996, this same survey showed that the three most highly sought-after skills in newly hired people were oral communication, interpersonal skills and teamwork abilities. Over a seven-year time frame, communication skills had become even more highly esteemed as predictors of contribution to the success of the organization.

A study of what organizations are looking for in the MBAs they hire shows that the three most desired capabilities are communication skills, interpersonal skills and initiative. Again, communication-related skills take the top two spots.

Now that we've covered the employer's point of view, let's look at what employees in the workplace are finding to be true.

A group of 721 CEOs (Margerison and Kakabadse, 1984) were asked about the most important things that they had learned to become CEO. They ranked communication first. Further, when asked about the key management skills needed to mentor others into senior executive positions, they ranked human relations first and communication second.

In 1989, Curtis, Winsor and Stephens surveyed 428 American human resources administrators about skills needed at different stages of a career. Interpersonal skills, verbal communication and written communication ranked as their top three. When asked what skills were needed to move up in an organization, communication became even more important taking, in different forms, the top five places.

Communication Expectations in Today's Workplace

The Conference Board of Canada, Organizational Performance Group, completed a study in 2002 titled "Leading from the Middle." The survey concluded that the five key personality traits and attributes required by middle managers in the future would be:

1. honesty and integrity,
2. sense of humor, ability to have fun,
3. humility, pride and empathy,
4. respect for others, and
5. trust.

This book includes these five attributes as part of the character requirements for healthy communication. It seems clear that on an increasing basis, employers want to hire employees with good communication skills and likewise employees want employers who practice good communication skills.

Reality Bites

I've worked here for four months and I am trying to understand how everything fits together. My supervisor is very patient with me but I still feel confused. I'm not even sure what questions to ask. I was trained to do my own job, but I have no idea what the company does or where or how we do it. I'll just plug along and try to get a grasp of the big picture over time.

Best Practices to help Clarify your Culture

Every organization has a way of doing business. Sometimes it's clear and sometimes it isn't. The more people understand the organization and what is expected of them, the better. Here are some examples of systems and processes that provide a framework for effective communication. Help to clarify your culture by incorporating the following elements:

An Organizational Purpose

- Provides a reason for being and a direction for decision making. May take the form of a vision, mission statement and/or strategic plan. A Departmental Purpose aligns to the big picture and provides direction for your team.

Goals and Objectives

- A collaborative development review system based on clear goals and objectives. Leaders work with team members individually to establish criteria for performance outcomes that align with the Organizational Purpose.

Leadership Practices and Systems

- A clearly understood and consistently modeled leadership style.
- An equitable and consistent process for hiring and developing people.
- Orientation programs to assist new employees in adapting to the organization.
- A consistent, constructive and frequent schedule for offering feedback, coaching and mentoring. Team members spend time with their immediate supervisor on a consistent basis for exchange of information, ideas and direction. Team members are encouraged to provide feedback about their leaders' performance.
- An incentive and rewards program that is team based in order to encourage collaboration.
- An open forum to suggest improvements accepted from all members of the organization.
- A Conflict Management Strategy that's collaborative and supportive.

Communication Practices by all Members of the Organization

- An effective Code of Behavior/Ethics which represents what the organization values in how people work together which often takes the form of values statements. Typically four to six core values establish communication expectations for internal relationships as well as interactions with customers, shareholders, employees, suppliers and the community.

Leadership Integration Model

Wendy's Restaurants
A solid set of values results in peak performance

"A great leader is someone who practises what they preach. They lead by example, create a sense of loyalty and teamwork, and are active in the community sharing their success with those in need." – Dave Thomas, owner (1932-2002)

Wendy's Five Values:

1. **Quality is our Recipe**
   The slogan wasn't just about the food served at Wendy's. It was also about the way customers were treated and it was Dave Thomas' life's philosophy.

2. **Do the Right Thing**
   Honesty, integrity, hard work, and giving back to the community were his values. Dave earned the respect of his peers and the love of all who knew him. He strongly believed that his values were the secret to his success.

3. **Treat People with Respect**
   Dave Thomas always remembered a name. He said it was the greatest sign of respect one person could show another.

4. **Profit is not a Dirty Word**
   He took pride in his success. Profit translated into growth and opportunity, allowing him to share his success with his team and with the community.

5. Give Something Back

He believed that financial support, or one's time or energy devoted to a cause, could make a positive contribution to the community.

Dave Thomas' compassion for adopted children led to the creation of the Foundation for Adoption, which most recently, contributed over $1 million (U.S.) in grants in 2002. His steadfast vision that every child should belong to a family has brought thousands of adopted children and families together throughout the U.S. and Canada.

Wendy's Results (U.S.$ – 2002)
- $9.4 billion sales system wide
- $2.7 billion in total revenues
- $219 million in net income

"Dave taught us some important lessons about quality, integrity, respect, pride and responsibility. These lessons evolved into the values on which we operate today, keeping everyone focused and providing a clear direction when making decisions. Each of us understands what's expected of us and how we're to achieve results. Within the organization, we operate by, 'Doing it Dave's Way.' It's all about living these values through our words and actions in business and in life."

– Patrick McCann,
Training Director, Wendy's Restaurants of Canada

Conclusion of Communicate Your Way to Success

Communication is unmistakably everyone's responsibility. It no longer belongs to the domain of leaders only. Everyone associated with the organization has a role to play in communicating effectively.

A strong communication infrastructure can provide access and opportunity for important two-way dialogue, can foster productive collaborative teams and can decrease the fear of risk-taking. Additional benefits are an increase in creativity, improvement in organizational efficiencies and positive impact on the bottom line. This describes a culture worth striving to achieve.

PRATFALLS AND PROTOCOLS

> "Always do right – this will gratify some and astonish the rest."
>
> ～&～
>
> Mark Twain

Introduction

Think about it – there's a protocol for just about everything from voting to formal dining. Organizations have protocols as well, but they mostly are unwritten. Protocols help us understand what to do and what not to do. Protocols provide a sense of safety and predictability in our fast paced workplaces.

From the Redmond Journal

If you think company protocols sometimes seem a bit stodgy or time consuming, be assured that they do play an important role in the smooth running of an organization.

When Catherine, a manager at a large food chain company, wanted to talk to the company president, she checked first with his administrative assistant to determine the procedure for getting in to see him. Likewise, when the vice president of marketing wanted to take his team to an offsite retreat, he too checked the protocol for doing so.

Protocols make for good company practice and they can ensure equitable treatment at all levels of the organization.

Over the Water Cooler

"I rarely see my boss and I have no idea what she thinks of me."

"Goals and objectives! Ha. You must be kidding. We just ship the goods out the door as fast as we can."

"I work here because I have to – not because I want to. With two years left until retirement, it would be stupid to leave."

"There's no one here to teach us the ropes. We're left on our own to figure it out."

"I have to be careful what I say to my boss – it could come back to haunt me."

Know your Organization

Reality Bites

One senior leader in a global electronics company once told me that he spent up to 60% of his time on corporate politics – speculating about how the company would be reorganized, who was seen as a hero and who was being pushed out the door, and finding ways to protect his division and his people. What a way to spend one's time.

Knowing your organization is a solid first step in finding pride and purpose in your work. Many people only take the time to know their job and immediate office surroundings.

Discover the following information related to your workplace:

- history of the organization
- organizational structure
- locations
- clients and or customers
- mission statement, values and vision
- the management systems in place that deal with issues such as salary, bonuses, performance reviews, policies for promotion, illness, and lateness
- reputation within community and industry

Talk to your Leader

Employees who are highly valued and who understand how their role contributes to the organization, generally experience higher job satisfaction. Here are some important questions to ask your leader in order to clarify your role.

Organization

❖ How does this organization live and measure the mission statement?

❖ How does my job contribute to the success of the organization?

❖ What are the values of the organization regarding:
  • work/life balance,
  • shareholders,
  • senior and middle management,
  • employees and contract employees,
  • customers/clients,
  • suppliers/vendors,
  • the community, and
  • the environment.

Expectations

❖ What are your goals, objectives and strategies for success?

❖ Are there team projects? What is the structure of those teams?

❖ How can I best support you?

❖ What would happen if you and I were to disagree?

Learning

❖ What training is available for my role?

❖ What are my opportunities for development?

Review

❖ What kind of feedback can I expect?

❖ What kind of feedback am I expected to provide?

❖ What is the performance management system?

Employees

❖ What makes people proud to work for this organization?
❖ What is the employee morale?
❖ How are satisfaction and commitment measured?
❖ What information is shared with employees?
❖ Is there an Employee Assistance Program? How does it work?
❖ When there's conflict with other people, what's the proper route for resolving the situation?

Tips for your success with your leader:

❖ Track your own performance. Keep track of your goals, objectives and the results that you obtain.
❖ Keep copies of letters of recommendation as well as information regarding what you've learned on the job.
❖ Ensure that you have regular meetings with your leader so that you can inform him/her of your progress, roadblocks and learning.
❖ Support your supervisors or leaders. Try to find ways to focus on their positive qualities and recognize and reinforce those qualities as you expect them to do with you. Offer constructive feedback judiciously, using a good structure (see SOLVE© in Strategy Four). If they're wise enough to listen to you, help them improve their skills. If they refuse your feedback, continue to treat them with dignity.

Find a Mentor

A mentor is a person (within or outside the organization) who can formally be appointed, or whom you informally request, to help you succeed in the organization and your work life. Typically, this person is not your direct supervisor or leader.

A mentor can:
- teach you the unwritten rules of the organization,
- provide feedback on your performance from a perspective other than your supervisor's,
- help you develop career opportunities within the organization, and
- coach you on how to improve specific skills.

A successful mentoring program includes:
- determining goals, objectives and timelines with your mentor,
- having more than one mentor, depending on what you're trying to achieve,
- using mentors outside the organization – some college and university programs offer mentorship opportunities,
- cooperating with the mentoring process by reporting regularly on your progress,
- showing your appreciation for your mentor's feedback and time, and
- offering to reciprocate your mentor's support.

Become an Ambassador

> When I do good, I feel good; when I do bad, I feel bad.
> That's my religion. – Abraham Lincoln

If you have nothing positive to say about where you work, you might want to reconsider your reasons for working where you do. Your opinion will influence whether people will apply for work, become a customer of, invest in or support community initiatives of your organization.

The Retirement Paradox

Perhaps you're in your 50s or 60s, only a few years away from retirement. You've done your time, put in your years, offered your best thinking to the organization and are ready to move into the next stage of your life. But you resist leaving the company for as long as possible in order to maximize your pension benefits. Now you face the dilemma of knowing that it makes no practical sense to leave early. You may also feel stuck, worn out and worn down. It's a common occurrence in today's workplace.

Reality Bites

He was sitting in the last row of the workshop and openly said, "I hate this company and everything about it. Twenty years ago, we were on strike and I will never forgive what happened to us workers. My boss now could not be nicer or fairer to me, but it doesn't matter. I will do everything that I can to damage this organization until the day I leave. If they don't like it they can pay me off and I will leave today". The people sitting around this man collectively rolled their eyes, but he didn't notice. He knew his open statements would go unchallenged.

This true case scenario is not unusual. While it was one of the most negative examples I'd ever witnessed, I heard from many older workers who quietly confided that they were exhausted, discouraged and unmotivated (and just as many or more, who are still energized and adding great value) and who were just hanging in there for a couple more years. One of the unsettling aspects of this paradox is that everyone associated with the organization suffers – the older workers, co-workers, leaders, customers, suppliers and new employees. A suggested approach is to find some meaning and satisfaction for the remaining years of your career.

Add interest to a long-standing career by:
- developing training programs for the people who will replace you,
- mentoring younger employees, or
- participating in opportunities that help transition employees, customers, and suppliers and yourself through change.

Conclusion of Pratfalls and Protocols

Clearly defined protocols are one of an organization's greatest assets. They frame expectations, model behavior, are proactive by nature, can encourage effective communication throughout an organization, and can prove fruitful to job and personal satisfaction.

COMMON COURTESY

> "The true measure of a man is how he treats someone who can do him absolutely no good."
> ⁕
> Samuel Johnson

Introduction

Courtesy in the workplace – is it a crazy notion or a secret tool for success? The workplace has changed so much in the last few years that it's become a challenge just to describe the confusing mix of behaviors that we have to deal with on any given day. While you might believe that you can "catch more flies with honey," one of your co-workers might lead with an "iron glove." We all have different styles. How to make those styles compliment each other is worth examining.

From the Redmond Journal

People tell me all the time that they try to practice common courtesy in every aspect of their life, but often don't try as hard as they should in the workplace. They're not even certain why they take liberties with their co-workers, treating some of them abruptly from time to time. Perhaps it's the constant pressure, or the close proximity to each other's work spaces, or the amount of time that they have to spend together. Regardless, I know many of them would like to see co-workers practice the art of civility on a more regular basis.

Over the Water Cooler

"No one ever answers the telephone any more!"

"My boss sent me an email five minutes ago and can't understand why I haven't read it yet."

"He just walked into my office and started talking – the interruption broke my train of thought and I had to start my calculations all over."

"Her cell phone rings at least three times during every meeting."

"No one ever says hello – they just start asking me for stuff before I even have my coat off."

Courtesy at Work

Our workplace is part of our life and practicing courtesy helps manage our expectations and frustrations.

Top Ten Courteous Behaviors

1. Say hello to people when you first see them at work. Say goodbye as you leave. The rest of the day nod or smile to acknowledge them as you meet.
2. Learn people's names. Spell and pronounce them correctly.
3. Ask people what's expected regarding office etiquette. There may be an "open door" policy or there may be a "knock first" policy.
4. Return phone calls within 24 hours.
5. Ask permission before "borrowing" from another person's desk.
6. Turn your cell phone off while talking to other people or while in a meeting.
7. Answer your phone when you're available and use words and a tone that demonstrate you're interested in speaking to the caller. Voice mail is not a permanent solution!
8. Respect privacy for documents or work visible on someone's desk.
9. When interacting with a customer, talk to that person and only that person.
10. If you need to take supplies from the company, ensure you check the protocol for doing so.

Risky Business

Leaders Beware! These are some statements that can take you places you would rather not go.
* Do what I say, not what I do.
* You can do better than this.
* I don't care why it happened.
* I should fire you for this.
* I'll do the thinking around here.
* I haven't got time to listen to you.
* I don't pay you to think.
* It's my way or the highway.

Teammates! Reflect long and hard before you say something like this to your leader.
* You're the one being paid the big bucks.
* I do a job. You're the one who's paid to be responsible.
* I leave exactly at 4:30.
* Fire me if you don't like it. I'll take a pay out.
* You didn't explain it correctly.
* I worked on this project all night.

Alert Signals! These statements have been reported to raise hackles on anyone hearing them!
* Can I be honest with you?
* Let me tell you what you think.
* Let me tell you your motive.
* My perspective is the only perspective.
* It's all your fault.
* I never apologize. I'm too proud for that.
* I'm right and you're wrong.
* You need to change and then everything will be fine.
* You're the problem.
* I don't care what you think, but I'll tell you what I think.

Electronic Courtesy

Email and other electronic devices have infiltrated our lives. Consider using these guidelines when communicating electronically.

- Be brief and to the point.
- Address people respectfully as you would in person using their surname if that's expected.
- Offer a pleasant introduction at the beginning of an email.
- Resist the temptation to use capitalized letters and exclamation marks if you're trying to indicate your displeasure or urgency. If the message is of a time-sensitive nature, use the phone.
- When the situation is particularly sensitive or if there's significant room for misinterpretation, refrain from using email. Speak with the person directly.
- Think carefully before copying others in an email because:
  - it's not always the best communication method for "covering your butt."
  - not everyone copied may want his/her email address shared by others, and
  - there could be a reference to sensitive information from a previous email, which isn't to be shared in an email sent to a number of people.
- When sending emails to a number of people, be specific in the action that you're requiring of each person.

Be Politically Astute

- Ensure that your decisions align with the purpose and values of the organization.
- Don't speculate with others about office changes. If it's appropriate, ask your leader for his/her insight or explanation.
- If you have something to say about someone, say it directly to him/her.
- Listen to the people whom you trust, who are honorable and who have integrity.
- Choose your "mountain to die on" carefully. You can't champion every cause. If a decision violates your personal value system, you don't have to participate.
- Discreetly investigate the politics of the organization before you start your job.
- If you aren't sure that something you've been asked to do is the right thing for the organization, then don't do it. Discuss your concerns with someone you trust.
- Treat everyone in the organization with dignity and in a consistent manner.

Conclusion of Common Courtesy

We work in busy, challenging environments that often seem impersonal and harsh. The human touch can make it more enjoyable. Courtesy clarifies the rules of engagement on a personal level. You'll no doubt enjoy being treated courteously at work and the people around you will enjoy your efforts of courtesy towards them.

GOOD CHEER

"The most wasted of all days is one without laughter."
_◆_
e.e. cummings

Introduction

The innocent question, "So how was your day?" can
often open the door to a reaction that describes your
work day in less than glowing terms. You spend the
majority of your life at work, so you might as well enjoy
it. Oddly enough, the more you enjoy it, the more
successful you'll be. Doing what you like, doing it well
and enjoying the journey is a far better way to go
through life.

From the Redmond Journal

After a downturn in the economy, extraordinary stress levels hit a financial institution in Montreal very hard. Absenteeism was up, low morale had set in and one recent MBA graduate blurted out during one of my training sessions, "I can't stand this place. I just want to work in a hardware store selling widgets. Or maybe I'll car jockey for the dealership across the street." When asked to expand on the cause of his frustration, I learned that pressure was taking a toll on everyone and employees felt invisible and unappreciated – a situation that added to an already stressful environment.

Over the Water Cooler

"He makes us laugh just at the right moment and all the tension disappears."

"It feels so good to laugh – it feels like we can work through anything."

"We aren't allowed to laugh at work – we were told it's disruptive."

"I don't know what it is, but after we've had a good belly laugh we seem to be more energized."

"I've never seen him smile. He looks as though he's in constant pain."

Have a Laugh at Work

Laughing is both good for you as an individual and as an employee. It benefits you physically, emotionally and physiologically. Laughter can help fight disease and improve your health. When you laugh, your blood pressure is lowered as you increase your blood flow and oxygenation levels.

Humor and laughter on the job decrease stress and tension. Laughter allows people to be more open to positive messages and more engaged with their workplace and their colleagues.

- Use humor generously but carefully. Sarcasm or humor that hurts is not funny.
- Laugh with yourself but not at yourself. When you put yourself down, you give others the green light to do the same. You won't be pleased with the results. However, taking yourself lightly, once in a while, can be a sign of humility and humanity.
- Tell a joke, or ask if someone else can do so, when there's tension in the air. Laughing together gives you time to breathe and take a break from what's happening.
- Incorporate appropriate humor into presentations, training sessions and other events to break monotony for participants.
- Ensure that jokes and humorous comments don't infringe on anyone's culture, gender or religion. Use a lot of common sense when offering humor.

Conclusion of Good Cheer

Look for what's good in your colleagues and in your organization. Enjoy the sense of humor of others and let others enjoy your sense of humor. Fun and joy are very attractive qualities for any environment, including the workplace.

Reality Bites

We looked forward to Friday mornings for more reasons than one. Every Friday morning our boss gathered us together and acted out the highlights of the Thursday night Seinfield show. What a hoot! It was a great way to start the day... and end the week. I suspect that one of the reasons we worked so well as a team was because of the joy and camaraderie that we felt on those Friday mornings, and had a leader who knew how to keep the air light.

YOU AND YOUR TEAM

"Never tell people how to do things. Tell them what you want to achieve and they will surprise you with their ingenuity."

~&~

George S. Patton

INTRODUCTION

Imagine if everyone who works for, or who is associated with, your organization worked toward the same goal. Imagine the energy, focus and achievement that would suddenly be possible. Contrast this with the sad reality that exists in many workplaces where people have to shore up their strength just to get through the difficulties and drudgery of another day, working alone in isolation from their co-workers. Working together is better.

From the Redmond Journal

Isn't it perfectly delightful to work with someone who really knows the meaning of "team?"

Everyone wanted to work with Sharee, a woman with integrity, compassion and sincerity. When she committed to a deadline, she kept it. When there were problems, she looked for solutions. When she got recognition, she insisted her colleagues be recognized also. And when someone needed help, she pitched in. It was all so simple – and so effective.

Over the Water Cooler

"We have no idea what other departments are doing – we just focus on our own priorities."

"We compete for the money and resources that are available. I'm lucky, we have an aggressive boss, so we get more than our share of the pie."

"It's called a team, but no one knows what's really going on. Most of the time people don't show up for meetings, so we don't know if their work is done or not."

"Accountable? You have to be kidding. How can I be accountable when I don't know what I'm accountable for? Who's going to hold me accountable anyway?"

The Need for Collaboration

As humans we have been programmed to survive on our own. By nature, we're not pack-driven. Consequently, it's been a tricky business to move from "fending for ourselves" to working as a team. Understandably, the effectiveness of the collaborative approach has been met with some skepticism.

The belief, however, is that the whole is greater than the sum of its individual parts. Therefore, our organizations benefit when we have everyone engaged and playing on the same team.

Collaborative groups are of particular importance today for several reasons. First, we are bombarded with an unprecedented onslaught of information, and everyone in the organization has access to new and different ideas and insights. Second, our learning curve is vertical – every day. The simplest task, like setting a watch, is far more complex today than it was for our grandparents. Mergers, restructuring, joint ventures and virtual organizations all call for our best thinking in order to understand, and work within, the new dynamic of the workplace. We're also part of the global marketplace, interacting with people from different cultures and value systems. Our shared knowledge, understanding and insights are critical to the survival and success of the organization.

Reality Bites

We were trained in business school to be sword fighters, to do battle for our own division or department. Sometimes we would end up being slaughtered, and sometimes, we seriously impeded the other guy. Regardless, we viewed the organization as a battleground.

Your Perspective

The way you see the world is very much dependent upon your "filters," your realm of experience – your upbringing, genetic predisposition, education, gender, culture, religion, and country of origin. It's important to understand that your realm of experience produces your perspective – a unique point of view that's the culmination of all that you are.

It can be an enriching learning opportunity to listen to and understand the viewpoint of others. It also can be surprising. Make no assumptions and listen well!

Barriers to Hearing

Intention vs. Translation

Even when your intentions are good, your actions may be received negatively. For example, you may think that offering unsolicited feedback to your colleagues will help them to do a better job, when in fact, they may actually see you as being critical and arrogant. Yikes! How could they misread your intention? It's easy.

"Good intent" is not good enough. You must also be able to read and anticipate the reaction of others by being respectful of how your words and actions are interpreted. In other words, if your colleagues start avoiding you when you launch into a feedback session, take notice. Your intent is being misinterpreted. Talk about it. Explain what you wanted to accomplish and be prepared to listen to, and act upon, the response.

Benefits of Collaboration

Collaboration produces many benefits, some obvious, some subtle. Individuals are more motivated when they're involved and respected for the important role that they play. Trust is enhanced through collaboration because people know each other better. Decisions are more effective when they're made collaboratively because they've included more generous, diverse and varied perspectives. The organization is less "leader dependent" on a day-to-day basis, which frees the leadership to develop people, communicate more profoundly and focus on the core business.

The Shift to Collaboration

There have been many attempts within organizations over the past few years to move to a more cooperative culture. Continuous improvement teams, joint projects, quality circles and committees' initiatives have attempted to bring people together to enhance substance and depth.

However, the real shift will take place only when all systems are aligned to visibly support, celebrate and reward organizational success in addition to individual success. And while it is still entirely appropriate and necessary to hold individuals accountable and to recognize their contributions, the organization must benefit as well. As Coach Dean Smith said to Michael Jordan in his freshman year at UNC, "Michael, if you can't pass, you can't play."

The shift toward a collaborative culture can have its origin in many places – either from senior management or within an individual department. Management teams need to ensure that they model the kind of collaborative behaviors that are expected from all team members. There are many benefits of encouraging collaboration at the department level, including the fact that individuals regard their own skills and abilities as contributing factors in building a strong team.

Contributing to your Team

You know you're working in a collaborative workplace when:

- the focus is on both short and long term business results,
- roles are described as part of a team vs. individual targets and objectives,
- people are rewarded for joint accomplishments vs. individual accomplishments,
- decisions are made by the team, whenever possible,
- there's a risk-free environment for offering suggestions for improvement,
- diverse perspectives are solicited,
- everyone has a voice and is expected to contribute to processes and solutions,
- leaders model risk taking and innovation,
- the environment is inclusive of every person in the organization, including customers, suppliers, shareholders, and partners,
- there's an accepted and followed process for offering constructive feedback and dealing with conflict, and
- there's an understanding that learning comes from making mistakes.

You can make an individual contribution to a collaborative environment by:

- thinking about the organization as though it's your own business,
- ensuring that your value system is aligned with that of the organization,

- connecting your role to the organization's mission and purpose,
- ensuring that there's a purpose and process for projects, meetings and other initiatives,
- offering timely solutions and suggestions for improvement,
- eliminating assumptions,
- practicing excellent interpersonal communication skills in all your interactions,
- soliciting feedback from your supervisor or leader, direct reports, colleagues, customers and suppliers regarding your skills,
- developing a plan to improve your communication skills, and
- finding a coach/mentor to help you with your professional development.

Conclusion of You and Your Team

There's no doubt that the combined creativity of a group is more powerful than the creativity of an individual. This section targets some of the practices that individuals can implement to become an effective team player.

Summary of Strategy One ...
Clarify the Culture

Communicate your Way to Success

Key Thoughts
- ○ Good communication is a key component in organizational success.
- ○ Good communication is everyone's responsibility.

Putting it into Practice
- ○ Ensure you understand the purpose and systems of your organization.
- ○ Commit to improving your own communication skills.

Pratfalls and Protocols

Key Thoughts
- ○ Discover the history and key information regarding your organization.
- ○ Support your organization in every way possible, internally and externally.

Putting it into Practice
- ○ Clarify your leader's expectations of you, in terms of what you're expected to accomplish and how you're to behave while working.
- ○ Find a mentor to help you navigate your way to success.

Common Courtesy

Key Thoughts
- ○ Courteous behavior contributes to a productive environment.
- ○ There are guidelines to determine how to work together. The more explicit the guideline, the better.

Putting it into Practice
- ○ Learn and practice what is considered "common courtesy" in your organization.

○ Learn and practice what you should "never say" at work.

Good Cheer

Key Thoughts
○ Using humor at work contributes to a productive environment.
○ There's humor that helps and humor that damages – ensure you know the difference.

Putting it into Practice
○ Lighten up at work.
○ Ensure that you're practicing humor that adds to the environment.

You and Your Team

Key Thoughts
○ Organizations benefit from people working together collaboratively.
○ Everyone has his/her own perspective. One of the challenges of collaboration is to create an environment where everyone, including the organization, gains from individual differences.

Putting it into Practice
○ Speak up – your workplace will profit from your perspective and contribution.
○ Learn to work collaboratively with other people.

Moving From Strategy One to Strategy Two

Strategy One – Clarify the Culture suggests that you get to know your organization and understand your own role within it. The next chapter, *Strategy Two – Know Your Character*, focuses on getting to know yourself, an integral strategy in the *Rules of Engagement for Communicating at Work*.

Water Cooler conversations you'll hear as a result of applying Strategy One – Clarify the Culture:

"I believe people really pay attention to my ideas, so I'm encouraged to offer more improvements and suggestions."

"Our clear protocols eliminate the guessing game – we know how people are supposed to work with each other, and what to do if there's an issue."

"I know what my leaders and colleagues expect of me and they know what I expect of them. It's all been clearly discussed."

"We're encouraged to laugh and relax. Everyone knows that makes for a healthy, productive environment."

"We've learned to see ourselves as one company rather than different departments competing for a share of the pie and individual recognition. Our customers see only people who want to provide great service."

Strategy One – Clarify the Culture

STRATEGY TWO
Know Your Character

YOU'RE WIRED

"The test of first-rate intelligence is the ability to hold two opposed ideas in your mind at the same time, and still retain the ability to function."

~&~

F. Scott Fitzgerald

Introduction

You might not always know why you feel the way you do, or where some of your thoughts originate; however, the more you consciously reflect on your own beliefs and values, the greater chance you have of anticipating your reaction in any given situation. In order to better understand how you "tick" it's important to know more about the basic functions of your brain and body – the intricate and complicated interplay of thoughts, feelings, memory and physical reaction. Your physical reactions are often directly linked to what's going on in different levels of your mind. When there's a noticeable difference in the way your body reacts to a situation, or when the intensity of your reaction appears to be out of proportion with the situation you face, you're probably experiencing the result of a past event that has rooted itself in your subconscious.

From the Redmond Journal

"They're all very good at their jobs. Too bad that they don't work together very well."

If I had a dollar for every time I've heard that from managers across the continent, I'd have a lot of dollars! Just think what could be accomplished if teams of talented individuals could get along. Learning to work well together takes time, patience and a solid appreciation for the fact that we're all truly unique, complete with different values and beliefs that guide our actions, words and thoughts.

Over the Water Cooler

"I froze, I couldn't think of a thing to say."

"All of a sudden, this sarcastic, venomous retort just flew out of my mouth."

"I reverted back to being three years old and backed into the corner."

"I wanted to punch him in the mouth."

"I couldn't even remember the information that I just read."

More About the "Matter"

Human evolution has taken place over centuries, during which time our bodies and minds have adapted to our changing environment and have become more sophisticated. It's interesting to note that our brain developed from the bottom up. Originally, only small circuits existed on top of the central nervous system, which today is know as the brain stem. The brain stem is responsible for basic, life sustaining functions such as breathing, heart rate and reflexes. Our brain is programmed for survival, known as the "fight or flight" instinct, a centuries-old reaction which has allowed us to be the hunter, not the hunted.

The design of the brain is important to understand for the following reasons:

- You can't change your basic system.
- People feel something about everything.
- Feelings underlie and can override rational thought.
- Feelings have helped you survive and now are key motivators.
- You can only think rationally when your body is in certain physical states.
- It's a powerful asset to know what state you're in at all times.
- It's a significant advantage to recognize other people's emotional states.

A major leap in our evolutionary process came with the development of the "Amygdala." The Amygdala is part of the *Limbic System*, wich governs emotions and influences memory (There are two Amygdala, one each side of the brain). Specifically, the Amygdala is thought to be responsible for attaching emotional significance to events/experiences and helping you remember them. In the brain, the hippocampus (a memory structure) is situated posterior to the amygdala. Thus anatomy set the stage for the creation of, *Emotional memory*, where the amygdala encodes our experiences for emotions and sends signals to the memory centers of the brain. We are thus more apt to remember emotional experiences of all the events in our lives, both good or bad.

The Amygdala also acts as our protector, as it helps us evaluate situations according to our emotions and helps us decide if we should approach of withdraw from a given situation. It is the source of emotional impulse, and responsible for this "fight or flight" response. This part of our brain remembers many things of which we may have no conscious memory.

A next step was the development of the Neo-Cortex. Neo means new. The Neo-Cortex houses the prefrontal Cortex, which is the site of working memory. It keeps the Amygdala in check and provides cues to appropriate behaviour. This is the "rational, thinking part of the brain."

The Hijinks of the Hijack

The Amygdala has a mysterious way of taking over certain situations. It still tends to function as it did when we were hunter/gatherers, springing into high alert to keep us safe and reacting in critical moments. An Amygdala Hijack is our brain's emergency control reaction, carried out by circuitry that evolved in our brains millions of years ago. When we feel panicked, the Amygdala perceives that we're being threatened. Our heart rate increases and blood is diverted away from the brain's thinking centers to other sites, such as the large muscles, for emergency response. Extra fuel becomes available, in the form of blood sugar, and less relevant body functions slow down. Heart rate increases preparing the body for "fight or flight." When stress hormone levels are high, people make more errors and are more distracted and forgetful. Even something they've just recently read may be difficult to recall. Irrelevant thoughts intrude on the ability to think rationally, making it harder to process information. According to LeDoux's research, information can travel from the eye or ear first to the Thalamus, and then to the Amygdala. A second impulse travels from the thalamus to the

Neo-Cortex, the thinking brain. This sequencing means that the Amygdala may be reacting before the Neo-Cortex. In other words, in certain situations, we feel before we think. Our ability to think and reason is diminished while we're in this emotional state.

The Hijack Sequence

1. Information received through the senses and the Thalamus allows the Amygdala to constantly scan incoming information, evaluating the possibility of a threat, or need for instant reaction.
2. When the Amygdala sets in motion a response to fear, it sends signals to different parts of the body, readying us for "fight or flight." Hormones are also stimulated to provide alertness and fast decision making to the brain.

Rules of Engagement for Communicating at Work

3. Heart rate speeds up and blood pressure rises. Unnecessary movement stops and breathing slows. Some circuits rivet attention on the source of the fear and prepare muscles to react accordingly.
4. The Amygdala simultaneously causes a shuffling through of memory to gather any information known about this present situation. This process is given priority over any other thoughts that may be initiated at this time, so the Amygdala effectively blocks any rational thought about an appropriate response.

I Think I'm Being Hijacked

Reality Bites

Her face was beet red and her eyes were bulging out of their sockets. I didn't care. We needed to get the problem solved and I pushed on asking questions. Things went from bad to worse. I guess we needed to take a break before trying to find a solution.

If you experience an Amygdala Hijack you may have some of the following reactions:

- increased heart beat
- perspiration
- blushing
- increased energy/strength
- tendency to raise your voice
- tendency to become immobilized
- wanting to leave the scene
- hanging up on a phone conversation, or
- shallow breathing or shortness of breath

Your Neo-Cortex is Your Friend

Although it may not seem like it at the time, there are certain actions you can take to mitigate the effects of an Amygdala Hijack. It just takes practice and a cooperative Neo-Cortex, the origin of rational thought.

When Amygdala Hijack is happening to you:

1. Recognize the signs and emotionally take yourself out of the situation in order to regain control.
2. Breathe deeply.
3. Focus on something positive. Think about a person, situation, an item that gives you joy, for which are grateful. The feeling of gratitude provides a powerful counterbalance.
4. Be cognizant of your body's reactions for the next few hours. You still have adrenalin in your system and you may feel more vulnerable/explosive than you would normally.

The Amygdala Hijack Effect

When you experience an Amygdala Hijack, your body enters a state of stress, which negatively impacts your capacity to think broadly and creatively.

During an Amygdala Hijack, your beliefs, values, knowledge and skills become secondary to your need for survival. That can be a problem because when you operate on pure emotion, with a limited capacity for thought, you act out of character. When you act out of character, you're likely to say and do things that you normally wouldn't do. It's why you blurt out insults that you inevitably regret during an argument with your partner, your children or your co-workers. When the Amygdala Hijack effect subsides and is replaced by rational thought, an apology usually follows. Take solace in knowing that this happens to almost everyone, and there's a way to manage your reactions.

You Are What You Feel

Reality Bites

He had severe pain in his shoulders and neck. Finally he was off work for two months recuperating from a spinal fusion. During that time he thought about the pressure he was under and realized that the pain had been a warning symptom. He hadn't paid attention. He just kept working and ignoring the pain until it was too late.

Paying objective and focused attention to your emotions may be a new level of awareness and information processing for you. Perhaps you've learned that behaving in a mature and appropriate fashion means becoming well practiced at suppressing your emotions, especially in the workplace. However, suppressing your emotions is the equivalent of ignoring significant information and wisdom. These feelings are a source of information that's noteworthy on several levels.

Another perspective is that suppressing negative emotions is destructive to your health and well-being. Your body is storing these feelings and the consequence can be negative. Your mind is also the memory, which may trigger a dramatized reaction to a minor event.

Getting it Together – Mind, Body and Heart

You can gain valuable information about the way you truly feel by paying closer attention to what your body is telling you. Do you say, "I'll have those numbers for our Tuesday meeting," with an upset stomach and a headache threatening to develop? When you say, "I'd be happy to help you with that," is there a tightening in your stomach or shoulders?

Is your heart racing? Do these bodily reactions signal excitement, dread, fear, or pride in being asked? Listening more carefully to the messages that your body sends is a good start.

You learn to listen in a variety of ways. One way is to stop and notice the sensations you feel on a regular basis. The next step is to link what you're feeling to your reaction. Once you've noticed an emotion, you can choose a course of behavior that aligns with your intent.

Making sure that your feelings, reactions and actions are in alignment takes some practice. However, if you can do it, you'll inevitably feel less stress in your life. Recognizing the signs of Amygdala Hijack, and trying to align mind, body and heart as a counteraction, can be critical to maintaining good relationships with those around you.

Reality Bites

He was the smartest guy in our class all through high school. He didn't study, but got the highest grades. He won a scholarship to a great university, but after a year he dropped out. Now he drinks heavily, is unhappy with his life, drives a cab in his small hometown and has become a recluse. What a waste of untapped talent and brainpower. He was gifted with high IQ, but he wasn't paying attention to his EI, his Emotional Intelligence.

IQ, EI and Engagement Skills

In the last two decades the focus on interpersonal skills, relationship building and communication skills has been the foundation for hiring, training and managing performance in the workplace. The excellent research completed in studying the mind-body connection has helped organizations understand human behavior from a fresh perspective. We can no longer hope to "will" ourselves into certain behavior. We have to understand our will and its connection to our behavior.

Emotional Intelligence (EI) relates to our complex, multifaceted qualities, such as self-awareness, empathy, optimism, persistence, and our ability to handle ourselves in social situations. All are crucial aspects of our communication skills. EI offers new insight into what happens to us physiologically. Each of these areas is accessible to us to work on and to improve. How we monitor, learn, and change our EI provides a measure and predictor of future success.

Daniel Goleman has recently completed a series of popular books in the area of EI. His books include *Emotional Intelligence: Why it can matter more than IQ*, and *Working with Emotional Intelligence*. These works bring together all of the research previously done in this area and organize it in an easy-to-understand way.

Many experts have been working on various components of the EI puzzle for over 20 years. EI is now mainstream as more companies recognize EI as an important predictor of success. Here's an early example of the experimental stages of EI work.

- Long before the advent of Goleman's work, University of Pennsylvania psychologist Martin Seligman was looking at optimism as a measure of a person's self-worth. He concluded that the way people responded to setbacks, optimistically or pessimistically, was a fairly accurate indicator of how well they would succeed in school, sports, and certain kinds of work.
- In the mid-80s, Seligman was asked to develop a questionnaire to test his theory on people applying for insurance sales positions with a large insurance company. The company needed to be able to predict which applicants were most likely to prosper, because

they were hiring 5,000 sales people per year and training them at a cost of $30,000 each. Half of the newly hired people quit the first year and four out of five quit within four years. They quit because of the high rejection factor in the insurance business. With a turnover rate like this, the company realized it needed a proactive tool to measure the tendency in sales candidates to be able to handle rejection. Was it possible to identify which people would be better at seeing each refusal as a challenge rather than as a setback?

- Seligman's research found that when optimists fail, they attribute their failure to something that they could have changed, as opposed to some innate weakness that they were helpless to overcome. That confidence becomes self-reinforcing as they make the necessary changes in order to succeed.

- The company asked Seligman to track 15,000 newly hired people who had undergone both the company's standard screening exam and a "levels of optimism" test developed by Seligman. Some of the newly hired people had scored as "super optimists" on Seligman's exam and had failed the screening exam. The results were startling. This group's performance was the best of all the newly hired people. They outsold the pessimists in the regular group by 21% in the first year and by 57% in the second. For many years, the only way to get a job as a salesperson was to pass Seligman's test. The company couldn't afford to have it any other way.

Importance of Emotional Intelligence

Companies have historically hired people based on their technical skills and intellectual capabilities (IQ). The results of several significant studies state that EI abilities are at least twice as important as IQ combined with technical skills. The rules of engagement in this book are an integral part of what is described as emotional intelligence. Being aware of our emotions and employing sound engagement skills in managing our interactions with others are critical to our satisfaction at work and to the overall success of the organization.

"I know what I'm supposed to do. I know all the structures for saying it correctly. The issue is that I can't do it right all the time – nobody can. I just lose it and let my frustration out." Common comment as people describe communication challenges.

Reality Bites

The EI and Communication Connection

For years we've known that interpersonal skills, good communication and the ability to work cooperatively with others are critical to an effective workplace. These abilities are the result of high emotional intelligence.

If you have high EI, it means that you probably have the ability to know yourself well and can communicate appropriately during the myriad of physical and emotional states that you experience on any given day, and it also means that you have the ability to recognize the physical and emotional states of other people and can communicate with them effectively.

Conclusion of You're Wired

So now you can understand why "mind over matter" doesn't always work. There are times when your body won't let you override your emotions in favor of rational thought. Knowing that and dealing with it is an important skill that you can bring to every aspect of your life.

KNOWING YOUR INTENT

"Watch your thoughts; they become your words.
Watch your words; they become your actions.
Watch your actions; they become your habits.
Watch your habits; they become your character.
Watch your character; it becomes your destiny."

Frank Outlaw

INTRODUCTION

All aspects of the communication process require a great deal of careful thought to ensure that the message that's being received is the message that you intended. Learning to anticipate how a message is going to be received is just as important as the delivery of it.

From the Redmond Journal

I met a speechwriter once who said that when she was preparing material for the CEO, she would "see" what the audience would hear. In other words, she anticipated the reaction of the audience to the words she was writing in order to ensure the intended effect. Wouldn't it be nice if we had the luxury of being so thoughtful in our every day exchange of words with each other?

Over the Water Cooler

"That's just who I am – take it or leave it."

"Do I really have to pay attention to everything I say?"

"You're too sensitive."

"I'm doing what's important to me."

"I'm doing the best I can."

My Character

When we talk about character, we're really talking about the whole human being – who we are, what we believe, what we understand and how we act. The model, which was introduced earlier in the book, demonstrates the many layers that form our character, from a communication point of view.

The Layers of Character - A Communication Perspective

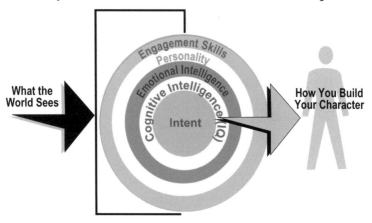

We Communicate our Character

Reality Bites

When we communicate we're demonstrating our character. "I believe that my boss wants the best for me. He cares about me as a person and is trying to help me do a good job. He tries to keep me updated about new activities in the company. I know that he's rough sometimes in the way that he talks, but I can overlook it because I know his heart is in the right place.

We demonstrate our character in the way that we communicate. And while good intent can overcome clumsy skills, it doesn't mean you can let your communication skills slide. Good intent combined with good skills makes for more effective communication. You grew up with beliefs about communication, whether you recognized it or not. It's an interesting exercise to reflect upon your own beliefs. And it's even more interesting to ask those close to you what they think your beliefs might be. You'll find out in a hurry if you're communicating honestly or not.

Expressing your Intent

Intent can be described in two ways:

1. It refers to our **beliefs**; our communication principles, values, rights and responsibilities.
2. It's defined in more situational terms, creating our motivation by focusing on our goals.

Communication Principles – *What we believe to be true*

1. Effective communication impacts every aspect of the workplace, and improves organizational results.
2. Communication skills can be developed and honed.
3. Positive intent is critical to good communication.
4. Collaboration, in most circumstances, is the best form of interaction.
5. Individuals with high levels of self-esteem are more likely to communicate effectively.
6. One's priority is to ensure that self-respect, personal safety and individuality are protected.
7. Individuals deserve to be treated with dignity at all times.
8. Boundaries are important in the workplace in order to manage manipulation and gossip.

9. Gossip damages workplace relationships and communication effectiveness.
10. Conflict, well harnessed, can spark creative opportunities and solutions.
11. Bullying is inappropriate workplace behavior.
12. Forgiveness is beneficial to all parties.

Communication Values – *Behavior based on the Principles*

1. Develop effective communication skills to foster trust, respect and cooperation.
2. Support the success and well being of everyone in and working with the organization, including clients, shareholders, and suppliers.
3. Work towards collaboration in interactions with others.
4. Treat people with dignity.
5. Provide an environment where people can intentionally improve their own level of self-esteem.
6. Respect the right of people to agree, disagree and make decisions for themselves.
7. Encourage people to interact directly with each other.
8. Discussions about people who are not present to defend themselves are not appropriate.
9. Bring differences into the open and look for creative problem-solving opportunities.

Communication Rights and Responsibilities – *Based on Principles and Values*

It's the responsibility of the organization to:
- set standards, provide training and feedback in the area of communication,
- ensure that every person is treated with dignity,
- support people in their efforts to improve their level of self-esteem,

- support an environment where people make decisions that they view as appropriate,
- determine that gossip which makes assumptions about the motives, thoughts and feelings of others is not tolerated,
- encourage people to interact directly with each other rather than through other people,
- encourage people to put their differences "on the table" in order to discover opportunities and solutions,
- ensure that the workplace is free of bullying behavior, and
- encourage people to forgive painful encounters once problems have been solved.

It's the responsibility of all team members to:
- develop communication skills,
- ensure positive intent in relationships and individual discussions,
- establish and work towards mutual satisfaction in conversations and agreements,
- treat every person with dignity,
- clarify understanding of self-esteem and work to improve their own self-esteem,
- respect the decisions of other people,
- not listen to speculation regarding the motives, thoughts and feelings of other people,
- not participate in discussions which defame a third party,
- directly approach others when there are problems,
- share true perspectives in order to enhance creativity and innovation,
- confront the issue, following organizational protocol if feeling bullied,
- learn to forgive in order to build good relationships, and

- understand that forgiving does not mean condoning, repeating or permitting inappropriate behavior.

The next influencing factor in our behavior is focused on our goals; priorities, objectives and standards.

Priorities – *What's important at a given point in time*

Your priorities are what you deem to be the important aspects in your work life and the urgency you give them. Some priority-setting considerations:

- If you're upset with someone, do you make time to sort it out quickly so that you don't harbor negative feelings, which could be damaging to both parties?
- Do you make time for those who want to talk to you when it's convenient for both parties to have a meaningful conversation?
- Do you schedule regular updates with your leader, clients and colleagues in order to ensure that you're communicating effectively, and listening to their concerns, questions and ideas?

Objectives – *What you're trying to achieve in a conversation or situation*

Positive objective
- You want a new supplier to be effective as soon as possible, so you provide information about the organization that's helpful in support of that objective.

Some negative objectives
- Co-workers don't provide feedback to each other because they're competing for recognition.
- You're irritated with your boss and create a negative version of an incident in order to discredit her.

- You want an elevated share of resources for your department, so you build a case with inaccurate information.

Standards – *Quality, quantity and level of excellence in a given situation or action*

Demonstrable differences in standards:
- Lou and George have finalized an action plan. Lou believes that the due date for his work is cast in stone and will complete the work on time. George believes that there's flexibility and feels that one more day won't affect the outcome.

Trust and Intent

You trust people who behave in a manner that supports healthy communication. This interaction involves all aspects of character, good intent, IQ, EI, an ability to project one's own personality and adapt to your personality. It also involves solid engagement skills.

Attitude and Intent

Your attitude is the manifestation of your intent which demonstrates itself through your behaviors.

Example one:
Paul has a great attitude. He works well with other people, is never moody, always approachable and works hard every day. Paul has a belief system that supports hard work, good team relationships and openness with other people. He's motivated because he believes that it's the right thing to do. His actions are aligned with his belief system. When we talk to people about their attitude, it's also important to be very clear about their behavior.

Example two:
Anne was a customer service representative with a negative approach to her customers. When talking to them, her tone was indifferent and she interrupted when the other person was speaking. When her supervisor talked to her about her attitude, Anne's response was, "My attitude is fine. We just have a personality clash." Her supervisor then described the behaviors that were inappropriate and Anne responded that she didn't like her job and that the work was beneath her and that customers were impolite. Anne and her boss discussed her beliefs about her work and Anne decided the job wasn't for her and resigned. Anne's attitude was a demonstration of her beliefs and unless she was prepared to change her beliefs, her interactions with customers would continue to be unacceptable.

Example three:
According to some of George's customers, he was too enthusiastic on the telephone. He spoke loudly, quickly and there were complaints about his overly exuberant attitude. He and his team leader discovered that George really enjoyed his work and was simply excited and energized when talking to customers. With some good skill training and self-discipline, George overcame this roadblock and became an outstanding customer service representative.

Conclusion of Knowing your Intent

It takes your entire "you" – your character to communicate effectively. Your intent is the most central component of your character. Everything you do and say reflects what you believe and are trying to accomplish. How your words and actions translate in the workplace can ultimately determine your success. We are all a "work in progress," fine tuning our intent and behaviors, in order to be as integrated, aligned and as effective as we can be within the workplace and with our co-workers.

YOU SAY NATURE, I SAY NURTURE

"There is an invisible garment woven around us from our earliest years; it is made of the way we eat, the way we walk, to way we greet people, woven of tastes and colors and perfumes which our senses spin."

~❦~

Jean Giraudoux

INTRODUCTION

If you're a parent of more than one child, you've probably experienced some significant variances in your children's personalities. One is outgoing, the other is shy. One is creative, the other is athletic. One eats fish, the other thinks it stinks. Go figure. Two children – same parents – same home – different tendencies. It's not so surprising, really. Each one of us is different – from our DNA to our fingerprints, and from our tastes to our styles and preferences. These differences make us unique. Diversity is a very good thing. But it's not such a good thing when we tend to expect other people to think, feel and react the same way that we do, all the time, in every situation. The challenge we face is learning how to respect, enjoy and celebrate each other's differences.

From the Redmond Journal

There are dog people and there are cat people. Usually, neither is too fond of the other's preference, but because both enjoy the company of a household pet, they understand the principle of the human/animal bond. We're complex beings, comprised of beliefs, skills and personality differences – some innate, some learned. Our greatest rewards come from being able to tolerate and celebrate those differences.

Over the Water Cooler

"Forget it – it's just a personality conflict. We can't work together."

"She just never sees anything the way a normal person should."

"He's the most disorganized person on the planet."

"Her style is just way out there. She should learn how to work in an office."

"Why doesn't everyone think like I do?"

The Person in Personality

Observing babies and young children helps us to understand that people possess qualities that are uniquely theirs. We're born with gifts and talents and sometimes they're embraced and sometimes they're squashed. Celebrated thinkers tell us that the best thing we can do for ourselves and for others is to mine our natural gifts and talents, letting them shine in the world for all to experience.

Reality Bites

They're twins, born within minutes of each other. One has red hair, is tiny, demure and loves all things pink. Her sister is constantly in trouble for one adventure or another. Her brown hair is generally in her face and she's covered in bruises. They're three years old.

Four Sides of the Box

For centuries, theorists, philosophers, entire cultures and psychoanalysts have tried to distinguish the characteristics of personality. In order to do so, many of these groups separated personality types into four classifications. It's interesting to note the varied classifications as they've developed throughout the years.

The four elements of earth, water, air and fire dominated natural philosophy about personality for almost two thousand years, aligning one's traits to these elements and to the 12 signs of the zodiac. The Greek philosopher, Empedocles of Sicily, was the father of this concept.

The eminent physician Hippocrates (c. 400 B.C.) of Kos, Greece, used four dispositions or temperaments to describe personality. They were Sanguine (optimistic), Choleric (irritable), Phlegmatic (unemotional), and Melancholic (pensive).

Native Americans divide the medicine wheel into four Spirit Keepers. The directions are north (mind), west (body), south (emotions) and east (spirit).

The four central desires of Hindu philosophy – pleasure, success, duty and meaning, describe the four aspects of human nature.

Carl Jung (1875-1961), in his work Psychological Types, said that we're born with certain preferences. They're our unique gifts. Understanding and respecting our gifts, as well as the gifts of others, adds value to our personality. He believed strongly that people should not be asked to change their personality. Jung named the four personalities as Intuition, Body, Feeling and Intellect.

Katherine Cook Briggs and Isabel Briggs Myers (1945) developed the Myers-Briggs Type Indicator™, which looks at personalities by considering the four dichotomies of Introversion/Extroversion, Sensing/Intuition, Thinking/Feeling and Judging/Perceiving. An individual chooses the side of each of the dichotomies which best describes his/her own preference in a given situation and is then categorized as one of 16 possible "types."

William Marston, a Native American Psychologist explored the meaning of normal human emotions by relating how a person perceives himself or herself in relation to the environment and developed the model called DISC which looks at the four categories of Dominance, Influencing, Steadiness and Compliance.

Dr. David Keirsey labels the four temperaments as Tactical, Logistical, Diplomatic and Strategic in his book *Please Understand Me* (1978). This work explores the relationship between the four temperaments and the 16 Myers-Briggs Types.

Don Lowry (1979), expressed his notion of personality through True Colors® which relates to the colors gold, green, blue and orange, to various tendencies in the way one thinks and behaves.

The research of D.W. Merrill and R. H. Reid in 1991, in *Personal Styles and Effective Performance* suggests that people exhibit four significantly different patterns of behavior, which have been summarized as the social styles of Analytic, Driver, Amiable and Expressive.

You Have Gifts

Unfortunately, the workplace is full of people who will try and mould, manage and control you into behaving in ways that are contradictory to the way you think. One of the keys to a successful work experience is for you to know exactly what you have to offer to your organization and to ensure that your gifts, skills and talents will be valued and maximized. Remember, you're unique and you have a great deal to contribute. A lot of job dissatisfaction stems from people being overlooked for their innate gifts and capabilities. Boredom and low morale are often the result.

Reality Bites

"My whole working life I've been told that I don't fit into the corporate world – that I just blurt out what I think and don't know my place. I always thought that the company wanted my best ideas, but now I realize that this isn't the case. They want me to 'think within my rank and answer when spoken to.' They tell me that creativity and challenging their way of doing things doesn't belong in their organization. I've been told that I either have to learn to keep my mouth shut or find another job." This remark was made by a creative, dynamic man who ultimately left the company and started his own business.

Some of the questions you might want to ask yourself in order to establish your preferences, might include:

- How do I want to organize my time and my work life?
- What activities do I really enjoy?
- How do I learn best?
- What role do I enjoy in the work group?
- How much attention do I pay to my intuition?
- Do I always need to have the facts to make a decision?
- Do I work best with schedules and a plan, or do I prefer being spontaneous?

Discover who you are. Find the work you love. Be with the people you enjoy. You're sure to benefit from a more meaningful life as you become astutely aware of, and aligned with, your true nature.

Ying vs. Yang

Reality Bites

She doesn't even use a time management system! How can we possibly work on this project together when there are timelines, milestones and deadlines that she just ignores? I'm frustrated beyond belief trying to work with this woman.

From the previous chapter in Strategy One, you now know that the group is stronger than the individual, particularly when the talents of each person are employed appropriately and wisely. As you begin to believe in what you can offer to the group and build on your own strengths, you can also encourage other people to do the same. That means that when each person's unique skills, talents and differences are valued and celebrated, the effectiveness of the group becomes heightened. When a group hums in this way, personality conflicts become an asset, not a hindrance, as they highlight these valuable differences. Ironically and sometimes, mistakenly, personality conflicts are often cited as one of the reasons that people don't get along well, when in actual fact, they can be leveraged for greater creativity, better thinking and more profitable, overall results.

Here are examples of what is labeled as "personality conflicts:" communication styles, indifference to colleagues, time management differences, corporate agendas and inappropriate behavior.

While these issues can be the cause of animosity in the workplace, real personality differences, as reflected by Myers-Briggs Type Indicator™, are described as the following: thinking before speaking vs. thinking out loud, relying on intuition vs. gathering the facts, and being spontaneous vs. developing a plan.

This is only a sampling of some natural preferences. And indeed it's not always easy to work with colleagues whose preferences veer in a different direction than yours. But I would encourage you to try to embrace the gifts and talents of those whose view you don't always share, perhaps practicing "tolerance" as one of your own gifts. You might be pleasantly surprised by the results.

Conclusion of You Say Nature, I Say Nurture

The only person you can ever expect to change is you. There will always be people you don't like and with whom you don't want to work. It's a fact of life, the study of many experts and the topic of much debate. Personality differences have been cited as one of the most significant causes of workplace friction. However, the way you choose to manage your personality vis-à-vis the differences of those around you, can be a learning opportunity, one that you can either ignore, therefore impeding your progress in the organization, or one that you can heed, encouraging your success.

SELF-ESTEEM AT WORK

"In a president, character is everything. A president doesn't have to be brilliant. He doesn't have to be clever; you can hire clever; you can hire pragmatic, and you can buy and bring in policy wonks. But you can't buy courage and decency. You can't rent a strong moral sense. A president must bring those things with him."

Peggy Noonan

INTRODUCTION

In all aspects of your life, including your work, you have to show people how you want to be treated. If you don't like the way you're being treated, then you have choices to make – choices that will improve your life and garner you the respect and treatment that you need for self-fulfillment. The more you become yourself, according to Nathaniel Branden, a pioneer in the area of self-esteem, the more you'll be comfortable in your own skin, and your work life will be more productive and enjoyable.

From the Redmond Journal

Every time he tried to assert his perspective he was crushed with the retort, "That's not the truth. That's not the way it is at all." It took him years to understand that "his truth" was equally valid and he did indeed have the right to his own perception. We all have our own truth and our own perspective. Don't let anyone take yours away.

Over the Water Cooler

"I'm a completely other person at work."

"I keep up the image that I need to have as the boss."

"I don't let my guard down for a moment. I don't want anyone to take advantage of me."

"There's no place at work for feelings. I'm paid to do a job so I just do it."

"How much abuse is acceptable in the workplace?"

Self-Esteem as a Component of Character

Reality Bites

Deep down he's really disappointed with himself. He repeatedly states that he's doing the best that he can, but refuses to talk about his beliefs or listen to how his words and actions affect others. He tells people that they're being aggressive with him if they try and talk about what's damaging to their mutual relationship. His excuse is, "Even the professionals disagree on the right thing to do," so he does what he's always done and is angry at the world for not responding the way he'd like.

Can this person get out of this trap? Of course, but it will take a conscious, focused effort and a willingness to give up the notion that the rest of the world must change. He's the only person that he can change, and by changing himself others will respond to him differently.

My Character and Self-Esteem

Your character is the culmination of your intent, your IQ, your EI, your personality and your engagement skills. Authentic communication is not a result of parroting certain behavior, but an affirmation of who you really are. Your character is developed from the inside out. The more you purposefully clarify and develop the layers of your character, the higher your self-esteem.

Take It with You to Work

Nathaniel Branden, in the *Six Pillars of Self-Esteem* says,

> "If I respect myself and require that others deal with me respectfully, I send out signals and behave in ways that increase the likelihood that others will respond appropriately. If I lack self-respect and consequently accept discourtesy, abuse or exploitation from others as natural, I unconsciously transmit this, and some people will treat me at my self-estimate."

In other words, the higher your self-esteem, the better you're able to cope with the challenges and frustrations of the workplace. The higher your self-esteem, the better you're able to treat others. By nature, you're going to be drawn to people who have the same self-esteem level as yourself.

Branden offers advice in the form of six pillars, or foundations, to help develop your self-esteem.

Pillar One:
The Practice of Living Consciously

To live consciously means to seek to be aware of everything that bears on your actions, purposes, values and goals – to the best of your ability, whatever ability that may be – and to behave in accordance with what we see and know.

Communication Thoughts for the Practice of Living Consciously

- *Clarify your beliefs* – discern what you believe regarding communicating with others.
- *Live in the moment* – focus on what's happening in the present vs. what's happened in the past, or may happen in the future. Avoid being distracted by thoughts that interfere with your ability to listen and understand.

- *When you're "in the moment"* – consider your objectives, priorities and standards.
- *Pay attention to the feelings you're experiencing* – they're important cues in your self-management which is a component of emotional intelligence.
- *Pay attention to the cues that other people are demonstrating* – adjust your interaction to support good communication – a component of emotional intelligence.

Pillar Two:
The Practice of Self-Acceptance

Aligning your behavior with your beliefs.

Reality Bites

When the question changes from, "What will they think of me?" to "What do I believe is the right choice for me at this moment in time?" you know that your self-esteem is becoming stronger.

Communication Thoughts for the Practice of Self-Acceptance

- Consider your self-talk. Are you encouraging or sabotaging yourself? Believe that you're entitled to respect.
- Believe that you're a unique and talented person who has gifts to contribute to the world.
- Believe that your thoughts are significant, your questions are important and your perspective adds value.

Pillar Three:
The Practice of Self-Responsibility

Take responsibility for your life and well-being. You're responsible to judge the circumstances and choose the most appropriate route for your happiness and self-respect.

Communication Thoughts for the Practice of Self-Responsibility

- Your first responsibility is to ensure that you're making the choices that honor your self-respect, safety and happiness.
- Don't allow yourself to be manipulated into behavior that you don't deem to be appropriate.
- When someone gossips to you, discourage the behavior and develop your own thoughts based on your experience.
- When someone asks you to rescue him or her, think carefully before doing so, or politely decline. Allow people to work through their own problems and challenges. Listen but don't suggest what "should be done."
- Don't blame others for your situation. Adjust to the people that you're working with by clearly establishing your expectations and boundaries.

Pillar Four:
The Practice of Self-Assertiveness

Self Assertiveness means the willingness to stand up for yourself, to be who you are openly, to treat yourself with respect in all human encounters.

Communication Thoughts for the
Practice of Self-Assertiveness

"Assertive people believe *we both count*. Aggressive people believe, *I count and you don't*, and passive people believe *you count and I don't*." Peggy Grall

- When you're treated with less dignity than you believe that you deserve, respond by solving it with the other person or by withdrawing from the situation.
- Ensure that you have equal air time in your discussions.
- Ask for what you need.
- Speak up and tell your truth. Your thoughts, questions and perspectives are of value to the people around you and critical to you.

Pillar Five:
The Practice of Living Purposefully

To live purposefully is to use your powers for the attainment of goals you've selected such as: studying, raising a family, earning a living, bringing a new product into the marketplace, solving a scientific problem, building a vacation home, or sustaining a happy, romantic relationship. It's your goals that lead you forward, that call on the exercise of your faculties, and that energize your existence.

Communication Thoughts for
Practicing Living Purposefully

- Establish communication and relationship goals.
- Confront relationships that are not respectful and establish boundaries that are appropriate for you in order to work together appropriately.
- Ask for feedback from people you trust.
- Identify areas that you'd like to improve and develop the skills to do so.

Pillar Six:
The Practice of Personal Integrity

Integrity is the integration of ideals, convictions, standards, beliefs and behavior. When your behavior is congruent with your professed values, and when ideals and practice match, you have integrity.

Reality Bites

We were told to ship defective product. I felt sick because I knew that our product had a life or death consequence. We were behind plan and the pressure was building. So I did it – shipped it out, and I've held my breath ever since waiting to hear if anything dire has happened.

Communication Thoughts for Practicing Personal Integrity

- Consider if the mission and vision of your organization are aligned with your personal beliefs. If not, consider where you'd be better suited.
- Ensure that your immediate work environment supports your beliefs.
- Speak up when people behave in ways that violate your beliefs about what's fair and appropriate.

Colleagues with Low Self-Esteem

Branden contrasts the behaviors of high self-esteem with low self-esteem which translate into the following workplace behaviors:

High Self-Esteem	Low Self-Esteem
Focused	Lack of focus
Seeks facts and truth	Opinion based and avoids truth
Clear and transparent	Vague and murky
Seeks new ways	Clings to the old ways
Open minded	Close minded
Values logic	Rejects logic

Clearly there are challenges for everyone, as well as the organization, when low self-esteem exists in the workplace. One key is for you to be true to yourself, insist that you be treated well, and insist that others also be treated well.

Self-Esteem, Accountability and Freedom of Choice

Responsibility
- answering for the outcome of a situation

Accountability
- accepting the consequences for the outcome of a situation for which you're responsible

Freedom
- making the choices that you believe are most appropriate in a situation

There's a particularly tricky balancing act in the workplace between the degree to which you're accountable for results and the leverage you're given to make decisions that can impact those results. In order to be accountable in an appropriate manner, you need to ensure that you're also free to make the correct choices.

Consider this example:

Georgia is a team leader and accountable for the outcome of a labor shortage study being conducted by a committee. Some people on the committee are not meeting their timelines to hand in work. When Georgia asks these people for results, she's met with aggression. The committee members accuse her of being insensitive to their workload and tight deadlines.

Georgia is reluctant to press the issue, as she knows that the committee members will evaluate her at the end of the project and she doesn't want to be seen as too demanding. Georgia feels pulled in two different directions because she's accountable but not free to do what's right – which is to assertively hold individuals accountable for their work.

Freedom to make decisions means that you sometimes have to make choices that protect your position and the responsibility you've been given. Don't let yourself be manipulated, threatened or concerned with how others may judge you. You know when you're doing what's right.

You and Your Organization

Reality Bites

I've been told to cut head count and I feel forced to let people go who have been loyal and very efficient. I find it unfair and it demeans me to have to do this. I have a hard time looking these people in the eye.

Sometimes your value system is not in sync with the value system of your organization. If you find yourself being asked to do something at work that you believe to be illegal, immoral or unjust, you're going to feel obvious pressure from an incongruence between your beliefs and the beliefs of your organization. Ultimately, you're accountable for the decisions that you make. And while it's often a very difficult choice, sometimes you have to refuse to take certain actions. Of course, there could be consequences, but consequences come with choices.

Your Building Blocks

You bring to every situation in your life and at work a set of unique and individual strengths. It's a key to your ultimate happiness to be able to use those strengths to your advantage. Feeling good about your accomplishments and contributions makes for a strong foundation from which to build your self-esteem. When an organization values and recognizes your strengths, you'll naturally become motivated to learn and to become more successful, ultimately benefiting the entire organization.

Conclusion of Self-Esteem at Work

Your own self-esteem plays a critical role in the quality of your engagement skills and is very much connected to how you work and the level of enjoyment you experience. The more intentional you are about discovering and enhancing your level of self-esteem, the better off you and your workplace will be.

Summary of Strategy Two …
Know Your Character
You're Wired

Key Thoughts

- ○ Your brain and body developed in a manner to protect you. Emotions can override our rational, thinking "brain" and cause us to behave in ways that are disappointing. You can learn to recognize and manage your emotional reaction.
- ○ It contributes to interactions to observe the emotional state of another person and adjust your interaction in order to lead to the best outcome possible.

Putting it into Practice

- ○ The next time that you feel that "you're losing control" notice your physical reactions. Is your breathing quick and shallow? Are you perspiring?
- ○ When you're having a physical reaction like the one above, stop. Remove yourself (if possible) from the situation. Record what triggered this reaction. Record what calmed you down and how long it took before you felt "back to normal."

Knowing Your Intent

Key Thoughts

- ○ Your intent is the heart of the matter. Your beliefs – principles, values, rights and responsibilities strongly influence the way you behave.
- ○ Your goals – priorities, objectives and standards, which are more situational, also influence your choices, words and actions.

Putting it into Practice

- ○ Examine your intent. Objectively sort through what you believe to true and appropriate.

○ Become clear about what's important to you in the moment, and what you're trying to achieve in any sensitive conversation or situation.

You Say Nature, I Say Nurture

Key Thoughts
○ You were born with certain preferences and gifts. Your job is to become the best "you" possible.
○ Each of us is unique. The challenge and the richness comes from understanding, embracing and combining our differences.

Putting it into Practice
○ Learn more about yourself – your preferences, talents and gifts. What do you truly enjoy? What do you feel passionate about?
○ Observe the differences in other people. How do you cope with those differences? Is it a source of irritation or does it lead to creative, multi-dimensional solutions? Look for ways to capitalize on the differences.

Self Esteem at Work

Key Thoughts
○ The higher your level of self-esteem, the more you'll enjoy your colleagues and your work.
○ We can increase our level of self-esteem through self-knowledge and focused effort.

Putting it into Practice
○ Review the concepts of self-esteem and evaluate your own level. Work with trusted colleagues to gain insight.
○ Focus on one of the concepts at a time and practice the "communication thoughts" to develop more skill in each area.

Moving from Strategy Two to Strategy Three

In *Strategy Two – Know Your Character*, we've covered a broad range of issues, ranging from the anatomy of the brain to the components of self-esteem and character. In the next chapter, *Strategy Three – Respect Yourself* we start looking at engagement skills, and there's no better place to start, than with an examination of how you treat yourself.

Water Cooler conversations that you'll hear as a result of applying Strategy Two – Know Your Character:

"I've learned to back away if I'm feeling upset and edgy. I've learned to leave the conversation for another day, when I can bring a fresher focus on listening and finding solutions."

"I now observe people more closely. If they're starting to lose it, we reschedule the discussion."

"I've come to realize that there's no point in ripping people apart. Maybe in the past it made me feel like I won something if I saw a person degraded. I now know that no one wins when that happens."

"I was born with certain gifts and preferences and it's my responsibility to use those gifts to contribute to all aspects of my life, including my work."

"I've learned to appreciate the differences between people. Different styles and perspectives enrich our workplace as well as the products and services we provide."

"I've decided that I'll only work in environments where I'm treated with respect and dignity. Anything less is just not good enough. If I find myself in an unpleasant situation, I'll speak up."

STRATEGY THREE
Respect Yourself

WORKPLACE BOUNDARIES

"In my day, we didn't have self-esteem, we had self-respect, and no more of it than we had earned."

~ 🐝 ~

Jane Haddam

INTRODUCTION

Have the people in your life ever offered their opinion about where you should work, what you should wear, or even how you should talk to your boss? Have you had to diplomatically suggest that they should, "back off." Well, you're not alone. It's a delicate balancing act to stay true to your own beliefs while taking into consideration the well-meaning suggestions of others. Clarifying your boundaries with those around you, and then acting according to those boundaries, is a proactive, liberating move forward in taking control of your work life.

From the Redmond Journal

She was dedicated to her job – an excellent financial analyst; however, she tended to keep her distance from many of her co-workers. It was apparent that she wanted to separate her professional life from her private life, and she didn't seem to mind that others misinterpreted her distance as arrogance. But this rigidity damaged her working relationships. She was just trying to establish boundaries in the best way she knew how.

Over the Water Cooler

"I'll tell you what's acceptable here – who are you to tell me?"

"I was just doing as I was told."

"My boss made me do this."

"Everyone else is doing it this way."

"There's no way I can say no – it just isn't done around here."

Begin with Boundaries

Your skin is a type of boundary – a boundary between your organs and the world. Your skin keeps the inside in and the outside out. There's another set of boundaries that keep us comfortable, safe and demonstrate the respect that we have for ourselves. These are the choices that you make about how you behave and how you allow people to treat you. These choices say to the world, "This is what I want or need. This is what I will and won't do." For instance, someone may be standing too close in a conversation and it makes you feel uncomfortable. You have the right, and the responsibility, to ask him or her to move further away. Or someone might make a request of you that you don't want to comply with. It's your right to refuse that request.

Boundaries are significant and worth understanding because they:
- define you as an individual,
- define and honor your intent, thoughts and feelings,
- reflect the choices that honor your self-esteem,
- keep you protected, empowered and responsible for your own life,
- guide the level of trust and intimacy in your relationships,
- support your own unique way of seeing the world, and
- demonstrate your judgement regarding the appropriateness of your behavior and the behavior of others.

Healthy boundaries will keep your self-respect high, your integrity intact and your resentment level low. These choices allow you to make good decisions that are right for you, further bolstering your self-esteem. Your boundaries may not always make you popular, but stay true to them and you'll be popular with yourself.

Free to Be

It's not always easy to make the best choices, but it's imperative to make good choices as you're ultimately accountable. Ensure that you have all the information you need and are resisting pressure to make choices that are not appropriate for you. If you're feeling pressured to behave in ways that don't support your principles, values, and goals, then you need to evaluate how well you're maintaining your boundaries.

You establish boundaries to clarify and demonstrate your choices. Your boundaries allow you to live according to your principles, values and priorities. For example, your boundaries allow you to manage time and money as you see appropriate, or determine how close or distant you want to be with certain people. Your boundaries keep you safe and healthy.

Proactively establishing your boundaries and responsibilities helps clarify core, acceptable behaviors on your part and on the part of other people in the workplace. Good engagement skills will help to ensure that your boundaries are respected.

How Does It All Work?

Here are some examples of various boundaries, and the choices, challenges and decisions that you can make associated with each.

Your Boundary – Your Principles

Your Choice	You do not lie.
Your Challenge	You're asked to pad a budget in order to access more funds.
Your Decision	The decision may be to work out as accurate a budget as possible and monitor it closely.

Your Boundary – Your Values

Your Choice   You determine the amount of time you
                   spend working.

Your Challenge   You're asked to be available for work seven
                   days a week.

Your Decision   You think about what's important for your
                   life and what meshes with your value system.
                   If you're single and you're early in your
                   career, it may be appropriate to be available
                   to work varying shifts. At another point in
                   your life, your partner/children might take
                   priority and you might decide not to work
                   weekends.

Your Boundary – Your Priorities

Your Choice   You work with your leader/client in order to
                   set priorities.

Your Challenge   A colleague asks you for help and you end
                   up doing his/her work which puts pressure
                   on your own workload.

Your Decision   Clarify your work responsibilities.
                   Continuing to shoulder another person's
                   work clouds realistic work distribution and
                   can negatively affect your performance.

Your Boundary – Your Money

Your Choice   You decide the salary you need.

Your Challenge   You're asked to take a pay cut due to hard
                   times, but the leaders are not doing the
                   same.

Your Decision   You decide to discuss this issue with your
                   leader. If you're still dissatisfied with the
                   situation, you start looking for another job.

Your Boundary – Your Friendships

Your Choice   You decide whom to trust and to include in your circle of friends.

Your Challenge One of your colleagues complains that you're aloof and not a team player.

Your Decision You've listened to colleagues being overly critical of other people and have decided that it's unsafe to reveal personal information. Your response is to be friendly, to provide information regarding work and to provide positive and constructive feedback as appropriate. You keep an emotional distance that feels appropriate.

Your Boundary – Your Feelings

Your Choice   You decide that you'll base your relationships on your interactions with others.

Your Challenge A co-worker is quarreling with the supervisor and wants you to side with her in order to demonstrate your loyalty as a co-worker.

Your Decision You realize that this person is trying to manipulate you. You manage the situation by staying neutral and treating the leader as he or she treats you.

Your Boundary – Your Personal Exposure

Your Choice   You choose to whom you will reveal personal information, thoughts and feelings.

Your Challenge You're asked during a team meeting for your perspective on the team. You believe that the team is dysfunctional.

| *Your Decision* | You give your perspective, if you feel safe doing so. One way to phrase it is, "My view is that we must build trust in order to be a more effective team. Here are the behaviors that I believe we need to practice." Don't single out any particular person. |

Your Boundary – Your Physical Aspects

Your Choice	You decide who can touch you and how they are allowed to touch you.
Your Challenge	Someone touches you on the thigh whenever they're making a point.
Your Decision	You're clear and firm in saying, "I'm uncomfortable when you touch me when we're talking." If the person continues you say, "Please don't touch me."

Your Boundary – Your Physical Space

Your Choice	You decide how close a person can stand/sit next to you.
Your Challenge	A person is physically too close to you when you're in conversation.
Your Decision	First step is to move away. Second step is to say, "I need a little more room."

Your Boundary – Your Safety Risks

| *Your Choice* | You decide what work is safe and what work is dangerous. |
| *Your Challenge* | You've had minimal instruction but are required to work with heavy, dangerous equipment. |

Your Decision	You ask for safety instructions. If you don't feel you have adequate instruction, refuse to do the work. You could say, "I need to better understand the safety instructions before using this equipment."

Your Boundary – Your Health Risks

Your Choice	You decide what equipment/practices are safe.
Your Challenge	You're getting back pain due to constant computer work with a poor quality chair.
Your Decision	You talk to your supervisor and explain, "I'm experiencing back strain and believe that my chair doesn't support me properly. What are my options?"

Good boundaries help identify those times when you're responsible "for" a person or responsible "to" a person.

Remember you're responsible "to" other adults, not "for" them. As you want to possess good information and make the most appropriate choices for yourself, others have that right as well. Consider carefully your relationships and think about whether you're overdoing the "for" side of the scale.

Responsible "for"	Responsible "to"
Fixing You try to change others so that they perform the job exactly as you perform it.	**Encouraging Individuality** There are different ways of achieving a task or a goal. Allow others, where possible, to find their own style in executing assignments.
Protecting You don't offer your perspective about a group's performance and let the group members believe that they're doing a good job and behaving appropriately, when you know they're not.	**Being Honest** Tell them the truth regarding their performance. Support them but don't do the work for them.
Rescuing You either speak for the person, explaining what you think is really meant, or make excuses for them to other people.	**Strengthening** The person speaks for him or herself without interruption or help from you. If others have an issue with that person, ask them to talk to that person directly.
Controlling You try to manage communication between two people.	**Supporting** Let other people work through their problems with privacy and dignity. Coach the person or persons to talk to each other and sort through issues together. This is their relationship – the less interference from you, the better.

Measuring Your Boundaries: Healthy, Rigid, Weak

Reality Bites

"My work friends know that I won't refuse them anything. They know that I don't want to hurt their feelings and I don't want to fight with them. They know that there's nothing I won't give them or tell them or do for them, whether I want to or not. That's just part of being a friend." This person often complained about how her friends run her life and take advantage of her. She feels frustrated and angry most of the time, and having weak boundaries affects the quality of her work life.

Healthy
You're able to make decisions about your own actions and are able to withstand pressure when being asked to do something that you don't want to do.

Rigid
You keep people at a distance.

Weak
You often agree to do something even when you really don't want to. You succumb to the expectations of other people.

Boundaries and Trust

You're more likely to trust those who are well intentioned towards you – whom you can talk with openly and who will understand and respect your perspective. You make decisions about what to disclose to people depending on the level of trust. Furthermore, those who respect you will also respect your boundaries.

For example:

You arrive at work upset because you had an argument with your partner. When one of your colleagues asks why you're upset, you politely decline to offer any information, mostly because you don't want to bring your personal problems into the office.

If your colleague is respectful of your boundaries, you'll be left alone. If there's little respect for your boundaries, your colleague will try to pry further. The intention could be well-meaning, or it could mean that there's a high need to know more and your colleague cares more about his or her own need than yours. You recognize this behavior as inappropriate and may choose to distance yourself from the person.

Beware of the Boundary Breakers

Others may try to crack and invade your boundaries by:
- accusing you of being cold or selfish,
- telling you that they're hurt,
- crying,
- using aggression or anger,
- excluding or ignoring you,
- enlisting other people to put pressure on you, and
- threatening you.

The First Person is You

A communication technique that will help you maintain your boundaries is to speak from the first person. In other words, whenever possible, use "I" as in, "I ask that you don't swear in the office."

"I" statements allow you to take ownership of your feelings and opinions and compel you to think about your own perspective.

Using the first person is an assertive form of communication, allowing you to tap into your own internal voice, also known as your intuition. It may seem awkward at first, getting used to using the first person, but you'll find it helps clarify what really matters to you and gives you the power to ask for what you need.

When you use "I" statements, you're able to:
- report how you feel and the conditions that exist when you feel that way,
- be free of prejudice, blame, threats or attempts to control others,
- be assertive,
- inform others of your feelings, and
- avoid over-generalizations and stating opinions as facts.

Instead of saying it this way,	try this....
"We think that all meetings should be banned."	"I believe that if we have an agenda and ground rules, our meetings will be more effective."
"You always single out my errors in front of others."	"I'm embarrassed when I'm corrected in front of other people. Could we try to find a way that works better for both of us?"
"The whole department thinks that you're unfair and that you have your favorites."	"I'd like to talk to you about how work is assigned."
"You just butt into the lineup. Move to the back!"	"I'm next in line."
"I think you should try something different to get our attention."	"Can I make some suggestions that might help get our attention?"

The "I" versus "We" Debate

In recent years there has been emphasis on the use of the inclusive pronoun, "we." "There's no *I* in team," is a familiar rebuke. It's completely appropriate to use "we" when discussing the plans and accomplishments of a group of people. The "I" is used to offer your own opinion and perspective.

"I" Can Set Boundaries

Example one:

When people ask questions that are too personal...
"I'm not comfortable with that question."

If they persist:
"Please don't persist with this line of questioning."

Example two:

When someone won't take 'no' for an answer...
"The answer is no."

If they persist:
"Please don't ask me for this again."

Example three:

When someone tries to push your buttons to elicit an emotional reaction....
"I find this discussion inappropriate."

If they persist:
"I'm ending this conversation."

Example four:

When you're asked to do someone else's work...
"I'm focusing on my own workload right now."

If they persist:
"No, my schedule is full."

Example five:

When you're asked to drop everything and focus on someone else's timeline...

"I've prioritized my work and I'll be able to finish this by..."

If they persist:

"How would you suggest that I reprioritize my schedule?"
or
" I've got to get back to my work now."

Example six:

When you're asked how much money you make...

"I find that too personal a question."

If they persist:

"Why is this important to you?"
"I don't discuss my remuneration."

Other examples that maintain boundaries:

"Here's what I'm prepared to do."
"This works for me."
"This is information that's important for you to know."
"I don't talk about other people. If I have an issue with James, I'll deal with him directly."
"That's confidential and I'm not at liberty to discuss it."
"I hold people's confidences as you expect me to hold yours."

Sadly, there are some people with whom you can't win. That is because they don't play win-win, they play win-lose. Interactions are used as opportunities to paint you as a villain. Observe with a generous eye, but if this behavior is habitual, keep your "dignified distance." Keep your heart open to improvement from people like this, but focus your energy on building respectful and trusting relationships.

Respect for Boundaries Builds Trust

Building Trust

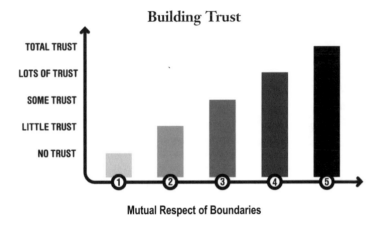

Mutual Respect of Boundaries

1. No Trust (Dignified Distance)

There's a great deal of prodding, making demands and manipulation on the part of the other person. You have to deal with those people who carry less than their share of work, and who rebuff feedback. Feedback to you is in the form of accusations and blame.

Relationship is: *distant and cautious – energy draining*

Interaction suggestions: *Treat the person with dignity, using very limited, careful interaction. Don't speak off the cuff. Use assertive language, not the language of feelings.*

2. Little Trust (At the Same Table)

You have to deal with those who do less than their share. Feedback is received defensively and provided to you aggressively.

Relationship is: *cautious and challenging – requires quite a bit of energy*

Interaction suggestions: *Use clear language and be firm with your boundaries. Speak from the "I." Provide feedback. Pay attention to all interactions.*

3. Some Trust (Across the Table)

Boundaries are sometimes respected. Sometimes there are problem solving issues, and sometimes there's some blame and some defensiveness.

Relationship is: *often enjoyable – requires focus and energy*
Interaction suggestions: *Stay firm, clear and consistent.*

4. Lots of Trust (Side be Side)

Boundaries are often respected. Feedback is received openly and new skills are applied.

Relationship is: *enjoyable with good exchanges – requires little extra energy*
Interaction suggestions: *Continue to enjoy working together.*

5. Total Trust (Heart to Heart)

Boundaries are clear and respected. Neither person is intrusive or manipulative. Both people ask for and apply feedback. Both parties respect confidentiality.

Relationship is: *comfortable, and energizing*
Interaction suggestions: *Continue to enjoy working together.*

Boundaries and Flexibility

While it's important to stand your ground, it's also of equal importance to be flexible when working with others in the workplace. You know that helping your colleagues and contributing to your team are vital attributes. However, this section does urge you to clarify your needs, intent, values and priorities in establishing boundaries to protect yourself and be appropriate. There are people who will try and manipulate you and exploit your vulnerabilities to satisfy their own needs. Your job is not to allow this to happen.

Conclusion of Workplace Boundaries

It's your responsibility to establish and maintain boundaries. Your self-esteem, work fulfillment, health and freedom to define your work life depend on this activity. Clarifying your thoughts and practicing the skill of setting and maintaining boundaries will only increase your satisfaction in the workplace.

Rules of Engagement for Communicating at Work

STANDING YOUR GROUND

"One person that has a mind and knows it can always beat ten people who haven't and don't."

~&~

George Bernard Shaw

INTRODUCTION

It's often difficult to know when you're actually being manipulated. Most people are decent and want to help others. In many cases it's appropriate and generous to do just that. Manipulation refers to actions such as being pushed, threatened, bullied, shamed, coerced or seduced into acting in ways that don't serve your best interests.

From the Redmond Journal

Colleen felt completely excluded from her team. They believed that she was playing by her own set of rules, and that her drive to be promoted was causing conflict and resentment among the group. Regardless of her excellent performance, she knew she had lost the respect of her entire department. It was becoming increasingly challenging for her to go to work. She knew she was being manipulated to feel bad about her accomplishments, but she also wondered if she hadn't manipulated others in an effort to move up the corporate ladder.

Over the Water Cooler

"You're so selfish."

"You're such a good friend. Thanks for talking to her on my behalf."

"She never helps me out. She doesn't care that Gloria is constantly giving me a hard time. I need someone to be on my side."

"She doesn't like children. She has none of her own and she won't ever give me time off for my kids' PD days."

"Management is really angry with me for not working overtime."

Transactional Analysis

Life Positions – the Fruit of Your Experience

Eric Berne's theory of Life Positions is a way of understanding how human beings view themselves and other people. By the time you reach adulthood you have a fairly entrenched Life Position. Early in life you received information that taught you about your value. Life Positions represent the belief or position that you maintain regarding your value and the value that you perceive in others. Understanding yourself and others helps you move to the "I'm OK, you're OK" Life Position.

1. I'm OK, you're OK. This is the best possible life position. We're adults and we want to understand the viewpoint of the other and find a solution. (Healthy Boundaries concept.)
2. I'm not OK and you're OK. I believe that you're smarter, more competent, more important than I am, and I acquiesce to you at my own expense. (Weak Boundaries concept.)
3. I'm OK, you're not OK. I'm right and you're wrong. Just do what I tell you to do and the world will be right. (Rigid Boundaries concept.)
4. I'm not OK, you're not OK. Neither of us is competent enough to find a solution. We just keep on doing the same old thing that doesn't work. (Weak Boundaries concept.)

Attack of the Manipulators

Reality Bites

My daughter Judy is upset over what happened this weekend. She was at the mall with friends and she saw Ashley, Barb's daughter. Ashley was with a group of girls and Judy wanted to say hi but she wasn't sure how Ashley would respond. So she just left and felt snubbed and upset all weekend. I work with Barb, so I know she can be so aloof and standoffish sometimes. It looks like her daughter is the same way.

When someone is trying to control your thoughts, feelings, and actions, you're being manipulated. Your choice is to decide for yourself how you think and feel about people, based on your relationships with them.

In the example, Ashley didn't know that Judy was at the mall, so Judy actually became upset for no reason. Barb may not have been aware of her reputation at the office. Neither did she know that her daughter's reputation had taken a blow. Rather than believe a story about another person, you can acknowledge the perspective of the speaker, but refrain from allowing their thoughts to influence your feelings.

Take note that this is only one version of the story. There's additional information that you, as the receiver, don't know. The organization is impacted by this kind of conversation which is gossip driven and based on a singular perspective. Unfortunately, in situations like these, relationships become stressed and collaborative opportunities can be lost.

So what should you say?

Possible responses for the receiver of a manipulation attack:

- **Barb to speaker:** "It sounds like you're upset that Judy didn't approach Ashley."
  or
- **Barb to speaker:** "What's tough for you is that Judy didn't feel comfortable approaching Ashley. Is that the case?"

The idea is for the person who is the object of the manipulation attack to seek clarification from the manipulator and try to bring closure to the issue in a calm and intelligent manner.

The notion of manipulation in the workplace is explored in the Karpman Drama Triangle as developed by Stephen B. Karpman, MD. This concept has been further expanded to demonstrate communication traps that exist in the workplace.

The Karpman Drama Triangle

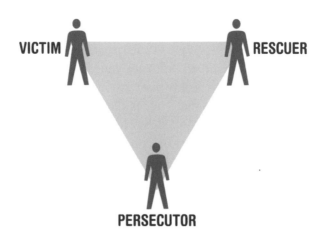

The Karpman Drama Triangle describes the roles that people often act out in various arenas, including the workplace. These roles are played out when people have hidden agendas, don't want to problem solve constructively, or don't want to accept a perspective other than their own. They're manipulating other people for dysfunctional, personal advantage and to abdicate legitimate use of their personal power.

The Rules of the Triangle

Round and Round We Go

There are two people at a time on a Triangle.

- The Triangle is either started with someone describing him/herself as a victim, looking to be rescued, or as a persecutor, looking for a target to victimize.
- Boundaries are necessary and appropriate and are established according to the situation. Healthy, mutually respectful boundaries are based on the stance: "I'm OK and you're OK." There are no boundaries in the Drama Triangle – inappropriate behavior abounds. Emotion drives behavior and those involved have not learned to think consciously about how they're behaving, nor have they learned how to self-monitor their emotions in order to achieve more rational thinking.
- People without boundaries get involved in perpetual competition to prove who's OK and who's not OK. The Drama Triangle struggle to be perceived as OK elicits extremely unproductive behavior. Any position on the Triangle is a negative position.

Role Beliefs of ... VICTIMS

The world owes me (I'm not OK – you're OK)
"You owe me."

"I deserve ..."

"I should have..."

"I don't have to do..."

"I'm above doing that."

"I did so much for you and you don't appreciate it."

"How many times did I stay late? I never get any credit."

"I'm so hurt."

"They're angry/unfair/mean..."

> *Victim Behavior*
> * take more than they give
> * don't answer questions when caught in a lie, exaggeration or attempt at manipulation
> * don't reach out
> * don't take a stand
> * pretend incompetence and weakness
> * believe that the world owes them something that they aren't getting
> * quit easily

Role Beliefs of ... RESCUERS

I'm here to save you (I'm OK – you're not OK)
"I'm more competent than you."

"I can take care of you better than you can take care of you."

"I know better than you."

"I'm stronger and smarter than you."

"You can rely on me."

> *Rescuer Behavior*
> * work hard to help other people – often without being asked
> * feel overworked, tired and sick
> * feel subdued anger

- don't have a "life" – so busy taking care of other people
- play the martyr
- use guilt or blame either subtly or obviously
- view themselves as responsible "for" people

Role Beliefs of ... PERSECUTORS

I push until I get what I want (I'm OK – you're not OK)
"If you can't stand up to me, that's your problem."
"I'll get them – one way or another."
"I'll get my way – one way or another"
"I like people being afraid of me."
"I'm stronger and better than they are."
"You did me wrong."
"You were going to fix it for me and you didn't."

Persecutor Behavior
- find fault and are critical of others
- lead by forcing people
- don't walk their talk
- sometimes display bullying behavior
- sometimes try to shame
- often blame others

Down with the Drama

These are some of the communication tactics employed by those on the Drama Triangle:
- winning at any cost
- violating the concepts of Communicating with Dignity (Strategy Four)
- valuing only one's own opinions and feelings
- telling as opposed to asking for information
- treating opinions as facts
- being overly emotional

- ignoring attempts to find a solution
- making assumptions about what other people think and why they do what they do
- involving as many people as possible in the conflict
- disrupting the workplace as much as possible

The (Dark) Benefits of the Drama

Believe it or not, there are those who thrive in the Triangle. The reaction they get makes up for something that they're not earning legitimately in their lives. Let's look at this role-by-role:

Role of ... Victim
Seeking...
- I get attention in my "poor me" role.
- I can control other people, making them do what I want them to do, so this makes me feel powerful.
- I don't have to face the perspective of the other person or face the consequences of my behavior. I find someone else to provide me with what I want.

Role of ... Rescuer
Seeking...
- People think I'm a hero because I'm always helping others.
- The "helper" role makes me feel needed and important.
- The "victims" will appreciate me for what I do for them.

Role of ... Persecutor
Seeking...
- People fear me and that makes me feel strong and powerful.
- Others won't criticize me because I attack first and they're busy defending themselves.

The Drama Disguise

People change roles in the Drama Triangle to maintain their illusion of power. People have preferred roles and preferred stances within each corner of the Triangle. These behaviors are fine-tuned in childhood and continue as adults. Once people are on the Triangle, they move around it and occupy various roles. The victim will become the persecutor by criticizing the rescuer for not fixing it well enough or fast enough. The persecutor becomes the victim of the rescuer as he tries to defend himself. Someone else steps in to rescue the new victim and another triangle is formed. And around we go.

Assigning Roles

To refer again to the example of Ashley and Barb, the speaker has slotted her daughter (Judy) and herself, in the role of victim. The mother is asking her workmate to become the rescuer.

> "If you're anywhere on the Triangle,
> you're everywhere." – Peggy Grall

The Impact of the Drama

Collaboration and effective problem solving suffer. Time and energy are wasted on emotional game playing, detracting from the work that needs to be done. If those on the Triangle are not held accountable for their behavior, they continue to behave dysfunctionally in the workplace.

Stepping off the Triangle

The goal is to function in an adult, mature relationship with your colleagues. When someone paints him or herself as a victim, adopt a Listen – Acknowledge – and Ask response (Strategy Four). If this doesn't work, you could say, "We've already talked about some of your options. Let me know when you make some progress."

Recognize when someone is trying to lure you onto the Triangle:

Are they behaving in victim, rescuer or persecutor role?

When someone is playing the "victim role" you respond in Adult-to-Adult (I'm OK – you're OK, responsible "to") fashion by asking:

"You seem upset. What solutions do you see?"
"What have you tried so far?"
"What typically works for you in a similar situation?"
"What next step makes the most sense for you?"
"What success have you had in the past with such circumstances?"

When someone is playing the "rescuer" you respond in Adult-to-Adult fashion by saying:

"I can take care of it myself, thank you."
"I have a plan to sort this out."
"I was just looking for someone to let me talk this out, I know what I need to do."

When someone is playing the "persecutor" you respond in Adult-to-Adult fashion by saying:

"This behavior is unacceptable to me."
"I don't allow people to talk to me this way."
"When we can have a problem solving conversation, please let me know."
"I'm only comfortable working towards a solution. Let me know when you would like to do that."

True Victims

Sometimes people are truly abused and therefore become real victims. If you observe this happening to someone else, you need to take a stand. Here are some guiding questions for you to ask yourself in order to determine the existence or level of abuse: Why can't this person stop the persecutor? What have they done so far? Does the person know that they're being persecuted?

If they won't take steps to help themselves, or their efforts prove fruitless, provide concrete examples to your leader, or your Human Resources Department about what's happening and follow up to ensure that the inappropriate behavior is stopped.

Enough is Enough – A Leader's Dilemma

Reality Bites

I'd had it. Joanne and Caroline both report to me. Joanne was being treated badly again by Caroline. Joanne had confided in me how hurt she'd been several times over the last year by Caroline's behavior. Joanne is condescending with Caroline, snubs her, treats other team members better than she does her, and is generally disrespectful.

I thought I might have seen examples of this at meetings, but nothing really flagrant. Joanne said that most of this damaging behavior happened when the two of them were alone. Joanne said that she'd done her best to talk to her, but Caroline just dismissed her. Joanne is a good worker, keeps me informed as to what's going on in the department and is really dependable. When I confronted Caroline, I told her straight out, "You treat Joanne terribly. You've deemed yourself superior to her when really she's the one that we depend on to get a lot of good work done around here. You have to stop treating her so badly." Caroline blanched, but denied everything.

She obviously didn't want to be a part of the team. What should I do?

What should the leader do, indeed? She definitely jumped on the Triangle. She was trying to rescue Joanne when, in actual fact, she should have encouraged her to take responsibility for the issues she was having with Caroline. The leader tried to intervene without knowing how Caroline was actually behaving, and also without knowing why Joanne was allowing it. Neither of these factors was her responsibility to fix, unless it was truly affecting work effectiveness. The leader's responsibility was to provide support to Joanne to help her resolve her issues.

It's always good practice to encourage people to work out their own challenges in building relationships.

Conclusion of Standing Your Ground

Manipulation does exist in the workplace. The key is identify when you're being manipulated and resist it. The Karpman Drama Triangle is a vivid model of how people can get caught in a manipulative web of counterproductive behaviors. There are degrees of these behaviors. Sometimes the manipulation is subtle, and sometimes it isn't. Regardless, it's one cause of low morale, dysfunctional teams, fear, and employee turnover. Setting clear communication boundaries is a key element for building positive, respectful workplace relationships.

Rules of Engagement for Communicating at Work

FEEDBACK:
THE ULTIMATE LEARNING OPPORTUNITY

"Feedback: The Breakfast of Champions."

Ken Blanchard

INTRODUCTION

Providing and receiving feedback is a good indicator that you're off the Drama Triangle. Receiving feedback can be a challenge, but it can also be very valuable.

When someone provides well-meaning feedback, it's relatively easy to engage in a good discussion. In this case, your role is to understand what's being said, present your own perspective and develop a mutually satisfactory solution.

When you're approached in a way that seems disrespectful, you may have a difficult time wading through your emotions to focus on the real message. The challenge will be for you to manage your own emotional reaction and transition the conversation into a positive experience.

From the Redmond Journal

When my twelve-year old nephew installed the latest version of Windows on my computer, I knew that life would forever be a never-ending learning opportunity for me. When I hear someone say that they don't need or want feedback, or that they want their learning curve to be horizontal, I think about all the growth opportunities that they're missing. I've learned to embrace the feedback process when it comes my way. And while I might not always agree with what's being said, I work hard to listen with an open mind and accept it gracefully.

Over the Water Cooler

"I'm not interested in your perspective."

"Who are you to give me feedback?"

"You're the problem."

"What makes you think I'm interested in your feedback?"

"It's all just too painful. I don't want to talk about it and I don't want to know."

Maximize the Feedback Process

From the previous chapters, you've learned that you're fully responsible for your own well being and for the choices you make. Feedback, whether you want it or not, is going to factor into every aspect of your life – whether you're learning a new sport, going to school, working in an office, working on your own, or raising a family. Learning how to receive feedback, so that it's always a positive experience for you, is a valuable skill.

Win-Win Feedback

The goal of the feedback process is to increase mutual understanding and to work toward a solution that benefits all concerned. In order to do this, both sides must:
- listen openly,
- understand and acknowledge the perspective and needs of the other person,
- engage in alternative approaches and options,
- work toward a solution that accommodates both parties, and
- agree to move beyond the issue once it's been discussed.

W5 for Receiving Feedback

Step One ... **Who**

Is the feedback directly from the source, or is this person a messenger?

Consider: If the person is a messenger, suggest that the "source" needs to problem solve directly with you, STOP here.
If it's direct information – proceed.

Step Two ... **Why**

What is the intent of the speaker?

Consider: If the intent of the discussion is unclear to you, ask the speaker to state his/her objective. If the objective is unclear, STOP here.

If the objective is reasonable – proceed.

Step Three ... **How**

Do you believe it's possible to have a productive, two-way discussion with the person?

Consider: If you believe that you can't have a constructive conversation with the person, STOP here.

Discuss what would make this a productive conversation for you: e.g. using the SOLVE© structure, focusing on one issue only, developing ground rules for the discussion, Engaging with Dignity and working with concrete examples. If you both agree to the process – proceed.

Step Four ... **When and Where**

Is this the right time and place for this discussion? Do you have all the information that you require? Does your emotional state support good listening and interaction?

Consider: If not, then reschedule the discussion at a time and location that better suits you both.

If you have the time, privacy, information and emotional state that you require – proceed.

Step Five

Ensure that the discussion is proceeding as agreed to.

Consider: If the process is not being respected, call attention to the fact. If there's no improvement, then reschedule the meeting. *Proceed by respecting the process as agreed to.*

Listening to Feedback

Reality Bites

When I'm approached with the notion of, "you are not good enough" I'm on full alert. Good constructive feedback embodies the notion that we're in this together, trying to help each other improve, learn more and find solutions. "You're not good enough," is a full frontal attack and can cause significant damage.

When you're receiving feedback, clarify what's being said to ensure mutual understanding. Rephrasing the message is one way to do this:

- "So what you're saying is that during the meeting, you believed that I was trying to put down everything you were saying. Did I understand you correctly?" or
- "So we didn't have all the information to make the decision and you want to review it now that there are additional facts. Is that what you're hoping to accomplish?"

Conversely you can check with the person to clarify what he or she has understood:

- "Please help me understand what you've heard me say. Perhaps you could just summarize the information briefly at this point."

Ask for Examples

When a speaker provides information that feels very broad, using words like "always," or "never," be sure to ask for specific examples of this behavior on your part. Behavior is described in terms of what is said or not said, done or not done.

The Choice is Yours

When you take responsibility for your own communication style, you control or own your beliefs, thoughts, feelings and behavior. When you allow other people to decide how you should think, feel or act, you're being manipulated. Feedback that's honest and fair can be helpful in providing you with insight and fresh perspectives. Over time, you'll learn how to judge your own behavior and develop principles and standards that are individual to and appropriate for you. Your own judgment is your guiding light and will help you to take full responsibility for your own well-being.

Games Adults Play to Avoid Feedback

Some people will try and avoid feedback through game playing. The following games are based on Transactional Analysis (I'm OK – you're OK) and variations of the win-lose mind set. These games thwart an honest exchange of perspective and the opportunity to find solutions to workplace issues. Beware of the game players!

1. **I'm a victim of your cruelty – lose/lose**
   (I'm not OK and you're not OK)
   "I'm helpless in this situation and you're being mean to me."

The person choosing to play this role is shirking responsibility for his/her own behavior.

2. **The best defense is an offence – win/lose**
   (I'm OK and you're not OK)
   "Forget me and let's find fault with you."
   Some people will try to be very aggressive, antagonizing the person providing feedback. It's another method of shirking responsibility.

3. **I'm in a power position and you can't touch me – win/lose**
   (I'm OK and you're not OK)
   "Who are you to criticize me?"
   Those in more senior positions within the organization, may use their status to mute the person offering feedback. Fear of reprisal in the form of scheduling, promotion or other work related issues will help maintain the silence. Everyone ultimately loses, including the company.

4. **I'll get you for this – lose/lose**
   (I'm OK, you're not OK disguised as I'm OK you're OK)
   "I'll tolerate this, go ahead."
   This person gives the impression that he/she is accepting feedback, then tries to sabotage the person who gave the feedback. The person who plays this game is defensive about receiving any kind of feedback, often providing aggressive feedback to others.

Conclusion of Feedback: The Ultimate Learning Opportunity

You're going to be more successful in the workplace, and in every aspect of your life if you can effectively learn how to deliver and receive feedback. It's important to understand how your words and actions are received by others, and it's of equal importance to help others understand the impact of how they're communicating with you. It takes time to develop this skill and to gracefully accept feedback. Be patient and objective. When you've mastered this skill, you will have acquired a valuable learning tool.

Summary of Strategy Three ...
Respect Yourself

Who Comes First?

Key Thoughts
- Boundaries will keep you safe and allow you to enjoy your work. Trust builds as we respect each other's boundaries.
- You are responsible "to" people, not "for" people

Putting it into Practice
- Establish boundaries regarding your principles, values, priorities and friendships (what's acceptable to you and what isn't.) Maintain your boundaries.
- Don't protect, rescue or control other people. Adults make their own decisions and require the best information to do so.

Standing Your Ground

Key Thoughts
- Manipulation is alive and well in the workplace. Be neither a manipulator nor manipulated.
- Beware of those who persecute, want to be rescued or want to rescue.

Putting it into Practice
- Recognize the behavior of the Karpman Drama Triangle (victims, rescuers and persecutors).
- Respond to the lure of manipulation in a way that keeps you off the Triangle.

Feedback: The Ultimate Learning Opportunity

Key Thoughts
- Feedback can be painful, but it also can be a tremendous learning opportunity.
- There are five steps in receiving feedback; who, why, how, when and where.

Putting it into Practice
- Ask for feedback; begin by asking people whom you truly trust.
- Listen for themes and trends and then consider making changes in your own behavior.

Moving from Strategy Three to Strategy Four

Strategy Three – Respect Yourself, you have reviewed responsibilities to yourself, how to avoid manipulation and the value of feedback from others. In the next chapter, *Strategy Four – Respect Others* you'll work with the engagement skills that focus on our communication with others.

Water Cooler conversations you'll hear as a result of applying Strategy Three – Respect Yourself:

"The answer is no. This behavior is unacceptable to me."

"I'm pleased to accept this job. It aligns with my values and the values of the organization."

"If you feel that George treated you badly, go and tell George, not me."

"What do I need to do differently to be more effective?"

"Thank you for your feedback. It helps me understand your perspective and we can continue to enjoy working together."

STRATEGY FOUR
Respect Others

ENGAGING WITH DIGNITY

"Too often we under estimate the power of a touch, a
smile, a kind word, a listening ear, an honest compliment,
or the smallest act of caring, all of which have the potential
to turn a life around."

Leo Buscaglia

INTRODUCTION

Do people earn your respect, or do you automatically
give them respect? Studies show that those who earn
our respect, keep it. Those to whom we automatically
give our respect, or who demand our respect because of
position, sometimes lose it. Is this true for you?

While this debate goes on, the non-negotiable
standard set by the *Rules of Engagement for
Communicating at Work* is that every person deserves to
be treated with dignity.

From the Redmond Journal

The most respectful relationships I've witnessed are ones where both parties have earned each other's respect through their actions – performing a good deed, defending a friend, offering honest feedback, listening with an open mind, defining clear boundaries or demonstrating integrity.

Over the Water Cooler

"You didn't let me finish!"

"I couldn't get a word in edgewise! He just went on and on."

"No, she didn't say that exactly. But I know that's what she meant!"

"I've given up. I'm so micro-managed that I've lost my confidence and my interest."

"Did you see the look on her face? It looked like she wanted to slug someone!"

To Engage With Dignity

Every person in every conversation should:

1. ensure that the timing and location of the conversation is appropriate,
2. allow everyone to speak without interruption, never substituting a word, or finishing a sentence for the speaker,
3. balance talking with listening,
4. involve all people in a group in the discussion and in creating solutions,
5. maintain eye contact with those speaking,
6. never intentionally humiliate another person, and
7. clarify the message by paraphrasing and repeating it back to ensure meaning.

Every item within the definition of "To Engage with Dignity" is designed to ensure that:

- ✔ the conversation is comfortably timed and paced,
- ✔ all parties express themselves and are heard,
- ✔ the exchange is dignified, and
- ✔ the actual information passed between the participants is received accurately.

Misunderstandings are very common. People say that they don't have time to slow down and really listen, but it takes much longer to correct a misunderstanding or undo the effects of a negative action, than it takes to listen carefully and to act appropriately in the first place. Misunderstandings also take their toll on your relationships with co-workers, making future communication more difficult.

Clarify Meaning

Reality Bites

It's happened many times working with individuals in conflict that an argument broke out over something someone "thought was said" that wasn't said or intended at all. How disturbing that conflict can erupt so quickly and thoughtlessly.

It's not unusual during a team meeting to hear people finishing each other's sentences. And it's usually the loudest, most aggressive person who dominates. A lot of good thinking is lost during these rapid-fire conversations because not everyone has a chance to be heard.

Here are some guidelines for ensuring that you've heard others correctly and have been accurately heard.

1. *Clarify* what you've heard by repeating what the person has said, in your own words and then ask for confirmation.
    "So, if I understood you correctly your point is that…"

2. *Clarify* what the receiver heard by asking for confirmation from others regarding what they've heard from you.
    "Please tell me what you heard so that I can be sure we're on the same page."

Your Body Speaks

The words you choose are often secondary to your body language. Your facial expression, posture, gestures, the look in your eyes, tone and volume of your voice, all convey meaning. Your words are important, but they're only one part of the communication package.

Reality Bites

Up to 93% of communication is non-verbal. Non verbal communication includes tone of voice, eye movement, posture, hand gestures, facial expressions as well as the energy and movement in your body. Eyes communicate a great deal. Strong eye contact versus shifty eye movement delivers two different messages.

Pick Your Spots

Reality Bites

The word goes around pretty quickly when someone is in the boss's office and the door is closed. We all watch to see who's coming out and the look on his or her face.

The location where you have sensitive conversations bears thought and planning. When you're working through a tough problem, definitely choose a private location. Often people are uncomfortable with public acknowledgement, so be thoughtful about the location of that discussion as well. Private discussions are generally a safer choice than public discussions.

The leader's closed-door office can signal to others that something is brewing. Consider what the office is typically used for and avoid this location if there are negative connotations for its use.

Timing Isn't Everything, But It's Important

Reality Bites

Fred always seems to approach me in the hall when I'm either with someone, or on the way to a meeting. He launches into a loud tantrum, using coarse language and a demanding tone. I try to set a time to talk to him privately and he accuses me of never wanting to listen to him.

The timing of conversations is also extremely important. If you walk up to someone while they're in discussion with someone else and demand to speak him/her, you may be disappointed. Where possible, it's always a good idea to plan a brief discussion, taking into consideration the other person's timelines as well as your own. You'll experience better results.

Fine Tune Your Tone

The tone and inflection in your voice can be very revealing. Patronization, boredom or weariness are some of the feelings that can creep subtly into your tone, but are clearly heard by the receiver.

Silence is Golden

Reality Bites

She asks me a question and then just keeps on talking. Or she'll ask three questions in a row and not allow me a second to think, never mind answer her. I'm not convinced that I'm even in the conversation.

Often your interactions can be too rapid to be effective. When you ask a question, wait in silence for the answer. Allow people to digest what you've said, or have asked them, giving them a chance to think about an effective, intelligent response. More thoughtful engagements will lead to better understanding and solutions.

Conclusion of Engaging with Dignity

At the heart of Engaging with Dignity is the notion that all people deserve to be treated respectfully – with kindness, understanding and tolerance. Remember, you show people how you want to be treated by treating them the same way.

COMPASSION

"Never look down on anybody, unless you are going to help them up."

Rev. Jesse Jackson

INTRODUCTION

We make sound decisions every day, based on our judgment. Should I let my son go to that party? Should I invest in the stock market? Do I enjoy working with that person? Is my boss fair when completing performance appraisals? Is it a good idea to repeat the information that someone confided in me?

It's your responsibility to judge the behavior of how people interact with you at work. However, it's not your job to judge them as people, and there's a big difference. We can find ways to care about people and to treat them with dignity and yet still deal with their inappropriate behavior.

From the Redmond Journal

I've reached a point in my life where most times I can be frustrated by someone's behavior, but can still value his or her thinking and individuality. I can care about the person while identifying and describing the behavior. It took me a long time to learn how to do this, but I have a lot less stress in my life because of it. I'm able to laugh more easily and I now tend to look for the positive attributes in most people. I believe that I'm learning compassion.

Over the Water Cooler

"I bet he treats his kids the same way that he treats us. Poor kids."

"She obviously thinks that she's superior to the rest of us."

"He's ticked off because he didn't get promoted."

"All she ever thinks about is herself."

"His problem is that he can't control his temper."

Compassion

Unfair Call

Reality Bites

I can't stand her. She thinks that she's too good to get her hands dirty working like the rest of us. She's arrogant because she has an MBA. I'll bet she's never worked a day in her life. I hear that she and the other new folks are called "over educated notebook junkies" by some of the gang.

It's highly unfair to make assumptions about what a person thinks, feels, needs, does or believes. Human beings are complicated and you rarely know what's going on in their private lives, in their hearts and in their minds. If you need to know something, then ask, rather than speculate and make a judgment based on assumptions.

Focus your attention away from the person and toward the behavior. Identify the behavior that's an issue, and if appropriate, ask the person to clarify his/her perspective to reach mutual understanding.

Unfair Call	"He's unfair."
Identify the behavior	Demonstrates a lack of clarity regarding goals and objectives.
Ask for clarification	"I believe that our situation has changed since the goals and objectives were established. May we go over the information point by point?"

Unfair Call	"She thinks she's above socializing with us."
Identify the behavior	A colleague doesn't offer to join you for lunch.
Ask for clarification	"Would you like to have lunch with us?"
Unfair Call	"The whole department thinks he's special and above receiving feedback."
Identify the behavior	People are too busy doing their own work.
Ask for clarification	"I have some feedback to offer, would you like to hear it?"
Unfair Call	"She's disorganized."
Identify the behavior	There's no clear plan for the project.
Ask for clarification	"I'd like to talk about how we organize ourselves to tackle this project."
Unfair Call	"He's still miserable because he was passed over for the job."
Identify the behavior	Person is withdrawn and quiet at work.
Ask for clarification	"Something seems to be bothering you. Would you like to go somewhere quiet and talk about it?"
Unfair Call	"She can be such a jerk."
Identify the behavior	The person used someone else's idea as her own.
Ask for clarification	"You know that idea was mine. Why did you use it as your own?"

Unfair Call	"He's irresponsible."
Identify the behavior	Turns in information late.
Ask for clarification	"The information was promised for this morning and I don't have it. When will you provide me with the data I asked for?"
Unfair Call	"She's always been a problem."
Identify the behavior	Timelines and standards have slipped from the original mandate.
Ask for clarification	"We need to talk about how to get this project done to the specifications required and on time. What are your thoughts?"

Play Fair

Reality Bites

I've worked here for a long time, so I know the whole history on George. He quit his job here about ten years ago and then begged to have it back. He tried working for another company, but just didn't cut it. Our boss felt sorry for him and took him back. He's been bitter about this company ever since.

When repeating information to other people, consider the simple, effective Rotary International 4-Way Test:

1. Is it the truth?
2. Is it fair to all concerned?
3. Will it build good will and better friendships?
4. Will it be beneficial to all concerned?

The person relaying the story about George may not have had all the facts. The listener could develop an opinion about George that would be inaccurate and unfair. Only George knows how he truly feels about the company. Nothing was gained by this conversation.

Conclusion of Compassion

Caring about people and dealing with contentious issues are integral to your work life and critical to building good working relationships. While it may be difficult at first to separate the person from his or her behavior, it's a valuable skill to learn. As you develop compassionate behaviors, you may convince others to act the same way toward their colleagues.

FOCUSING ON STRENGTHS

"There is more hunger for love and appreciation in this world than for bread."

Mother Teresa

INTRODUCTION

Do you see the donut or the hole? Is the glass half full or half empty? Is the sky partly sunny or partly cloudy? Are you an optimist or a pessimist? Your answers to these simple questions are influenced by the culmination of your life experiences. And your life experiences influence the way you communicate with everyone you know. Your outlook on life can affect your success in both personal and professional relationships. Everyone loves an optimist. It feels good to be in the presence of positive energy and creative thinking. Conversely, the feelings you get around a pessimist are just as powerful, but not as productive. Which characteristic describes you?

From the Redmond Journal

For over ten years I've asked people attending my workshops if they feel valued and if they receive the feedback that they require in all aspects of their life. I remember one man's response in particular. He said that his mother and wife were very generous in offering feedback and that he knew he was appreciated and supported. The vast majority of others said that they didn't know – that they weren't sure who thought they did good work or were happy to have them in their lives. I've also watched people squirm with discomfort as honest positive feedback is offered to them in these sessions. Isn't it unfortunate that we don't tell people more often what we think of them? A kind word is such a powerful gesture.

Over the Water Cooler

"I'm just a number around here."

"I have no idea what my supervisor thinks of me."

"I have no idea what my employees think of me."

"It's her job; why should I compliment her?"

"No way would I compliment my boss; everyone would think that I'm sucking up or looking for a raise."

In a Perfect World....

The ideal workplace differs somewhat from the reality of the workplace. But for a moment, just imagine...

- a company where all employees have a crystal clear understanding of what they're expected to achieve and are guided by a set of beliefs to guide their decision making,
- that if your leader is pleased with your work, he or she tells you quickly and with sincerity,
- that your leader sits down with you and finds solutions to problems in a constructive, positive and respectful manner,
- that you feel comfortable enough to provide the same positive feedback to your leader,
- feeling comfortable speaking up and stating what you see as helpful and valuable, without fear of embarrassment or ridicule,
- when there's a misunderstanding, obstacle or roadblock, sitting down with your leader and/or colleagues immediately, and smoothly working through the issue without fear of conflict or retribution, or
- your fellow workers frequently telling you what they value about you.

Sound good? Believe that it's all possible – definitely within your reach. It does require, however, that everyone in an organization, or on a team, understands, embraces and practices the same rules of engagement.

Accentuate the Positive

Positive communication in the workplace can have the following effects:

Increased
- energy for dynamic productivity
- team work
- harmony and good will
- enjoyment of work and the workplace

Greater
- sense of dignity and self-respect
- sense of security and belonging
- enjoyment in the workplace
- productivity

Reality Bites

The Canadian economy loses $11 billion a year in productivity due to mental illnesses and illness associated with addiction. A RAND Corporation study found that the estimated cost of depression in the United States in 1990 ranged from $30-44 billion. I wonder what impact more open appreciation would have?

If ongoing feedback is not initiated by your supervisor, it's your responsibility to ask for that information.

Revel in Recognition

Reality Bites

I just don't understand why we have to tell people that they're doing a good job when that's exactly what we pay them to do. I never hear a word from my boss unless there's a problem, and I like it that way. We coddle people too much around here.

The need to feel valued and to make a contribution rates high in priority on virtually every study of employee satisfaction. There are clear benefits to explaining to people the positive things they're doing:

Benefits
- Employees understand that they're valued.
- Employees understand expectations.
- Employees repeat the behavior that's recognized.
- Morale improves as employees are acknowledged for contributing to the workplace and to a team.

Why Do We Hesitate to Provide Feedback?

I've asked this question hundreds of times and this is how people inevitably respond:
- "I don't have time."
- "I don't know what to say."
- "I'm not sure how the person will react."
- "I think we might have to compliment everyone."
- "I don't want the person's head to 'swell.'"
- "I'm not complimented in return."
- "I don't want to embarrass the person."

Try providing more positive recognition to your colleagues and all those around you, and weigh the reaction. If you find that people value your effort, then continue. You just might discover the results are so beneficial, that you'll continue that practice for the rest of your life.

How to Provide CREDIT©

When offering feedback or compliments, be authentic in your use of positive reinforcement. Find the words that work best for you. Describe exactly what the person did and the impact of the action.

The CREDIT© format will help you focus on the critical elements of positive reinforcement.

C ircumstance, context
R ecognize, reinforce
E xactly what the person
D id
I dentify
T he outcome, impact

CREDIT© Considerations

Know the Facts ... The more knowledgeable you are about what the person actually did and the outcome or impact, the more credibility your feedback will have. Remember, you're offering feedback from your own perspective.

Here's how it works ...

CREDIT©

Circumstance

What was the situation, context, background?
"I needed help as I had a commitment outside of work."

Recognize

Reinforce behavior
"I want to thank you for helping me out with the schedule this week."

Exactly what the person
Did

What did the person say / do?
"When you agreed to switch shifts, it really took the pressure off."

Identify
The outcome

What was the end result for you?
"I was able to attend my son's last hockey game. I appreciated your help and I'll be happy to do the same for you in the future. Thanks."

Body Benefits ... When we feel grateful, we experience parasympathetic arousal, the physiological opposite of the fight or flight response triggered by fear or anger. This relaxation response is a broad, body wide response that creates a state of calm and contentment, which facilitates cooperation.

Timing is Key ... The rule of thumb is to offer feedback as close to the event as possible. Good timing adds to the significance of the feedback.

Speak to be Heard … Ensure that you ask about, clarify and understand the situation from the viewpoint of the other person.

Public or Private … Some people prefer to hear a compliment privately and some prefer a public forum. Consider offering positive feedback privately and if appropriate, ask the person if he/she would like to have the recognition repeated in a public forum such as in a meeting or company newsletter.

Body Language … Ensure that your body language and tone of voice align with your message. Face the person, make good eye contact, and use a tone of voice that conveys the meaning you intend.

Consider the Reason … When a supervisor compliments everyone for everything, the meaning of the compliment often gets diluted. You need to choose your compliments carefully. Whenever you see behavior that you value and would like to see repeated, you may want to reinforce it with a compliment. We all appreciate knowing what our colleagues value.

Documentation … When and where possible, ask for and provide written positive reinforcement. It's very useful for performance reviews, job applications, and references.

The Trust Benefit … When you're open and generous about letting your colleagues know what you value, you're contributing to a trusting relationship. It's much easier to problem solve with a person if you've built a solid level of trust.

Conclusion of Focusing on Strengths

Optimism and pessimism are often the result of the way you've been treated. If your actions and behaviors are positively reinforced, you're going to tend to be more positive with others. Optimism can be infectious. Try it!

FINDING SOLUTIONS

"Peace cannot be achieved through violence,
it can only be attained through understanding."

Ralph Waldo Emerson

INTRODUCTION

Just as positive reinforcement is necessary, so too is
constructive or developmental feedback. It's important
to be able to present your perspective, listen carefully to
the perspective of another person, brainstorm a solution,
and evolve an action plan together. The stability and
growth of organizations depend on the skill of all
stakeholders to deal effectively with roadblocks and
obstacles.

There are numerous benefits in being able to aptly
provide constructive feedback and collaborate to
develop solutions that incorporate the needs and
perspectives of all concerned.

From the Redmond Journal

It's imperative to deal quickly with situations that go wrong in the workplace. The tough part is that very few people want to play "the bad guy" by offering constructive criticism. Ironically, constructive criticism, if done with tact and professionalism, can be one of your organization's most effective learning tools. There's a great deal to be gained from making mistakes, and someone who is dedicated to his or her job will want to ensure that those mistakes aren't repeated.

Over the Water Cooler

"I tore a strip off him."

"I put her in her place."

"She knows, in no uncertain terms, what I think."

"If you don't like it – there's the door."

"The message has been delivered."

The Art of Problem Solving

It's a critical workplace skill to be able to sit down with another person and work through difficult issues. Remember, there are at least two sides to every story and your purpose in taking this step is to explain your perspective, to understand the other person's perspective and to formulate a plan that will solve the problem.

So often problems are not confronted directly. Some common responses for this are:

- "I might hurt the other person's feelings."
- "I don't have the time."
- "It might put a spotlight on my performance."
- "I'm fearful of the reaction."
- "I might be misunderstood."
- "There could be retribution for speaking up."
- "I'm not sure how to say it."
- "It's better not to rock the boat."
- "It might hurt the relationship with the other person."
- "The person won't like me any more."
- "Other people will hear about it and will judge me harshly."

While these reasons are very human, they aren't helpful and constructive. One step at a time, let's work to SOLVE©.

Fight/Flight or SOLVE©

In Strategy Two, you learned about the fight or flight instinct and your brain's capacity to prepare you for danger. You also learned that you have the ability to contradict your fight or flight instinct with rational thought. In this chapter, we'll refer to SOLVE© as the alternative to the fight or flight instinct.

In **fight** mode you might:
- become aggressive,
- defend a position,
- hurt people by damaging their reputation or their productivity on the job,
- blame, shame or unfairly judge someone, or
- manipulate a situation to benefit your purposes.

In **flight** mode you might:
- refuse to deal with the situation,
- go silent,
- avoid people at work,
- refuse to confront inappropriate behavior, or
- quit a job.

Using SOLVE© you will:

Solution-Focused Feedback

S pecify the facts / your perspective
O f the situation
L isten to the other side
V alue their perspective
E volve an Action Plan together

Here's how it works …

SOLVE©

S pecify the Facts

What was the situation, context, background, your perspective?
"I would like to talk about when we started the shift this morning
and I asked you for information about the machine."

O f the situation

What did the person say/do? What was the impact of the action?
What was the end result for you? On the team? Client? Organization?
"There wasn't enough detail for me to understand what I needed
to do to get it up and running. I ended up with a frustrating
morning and lost a lot of time."

L isten to the other side
V alue their perspective

Seek the other person's perspective
"What was going on for you when I asked for the information?"

(Listen, listen, listen

Test understanding

Acknowledge/Empathize)

E volve an Action Plan together

Seek an alternative, **ask & offer**	**The result of the alternative** **action**
"What can we do next time so this doesn't happen again? Your thoughts?"	"That will help me plan better."
(Listen to suggestion)	
"Maybe we should take a few minutes at the changeover and work through the details before the other person goes home."(your thoughts, if necessary)	"Let's get together next Friday and assess how well we're doing with this plan. Thanks for working out a solution with me."

Solving the Mystery

The SOLVE© process may look straight forward, but there are many nuances at each step along the way. SOLVE© requires a mutual, exploratory path and may take place over a period of time rather than be completed in one meeting. It may not evolve step-by-step, and that's fine. What's important is to ensure that you've covered all the key areas. The process relies heavily on the integrity of each person – the respect he/she holds for each other and the trust that has been built in the relationship. The contribution of each person is critical to reaching a solution for both parties.

Specify the Facts Of the Situation

- The facts are only what you know at a certain point in time. The other person has facts to contribute as well. You may have to do some research to find more information related to the situation.
- Your thoughts regarding the situation are also a critical piece of the puzzle. Your thoughts are your interpretation of what's happened.
- Your feelings are perhaps the most challenging component of this discussion and your openness will be dictated by the amount of trust you have in your relationship with the other person.

Listen to the Other Side

- Test your understanding of what is said. "Did you say…."
- Clarify using open-ended questions. "Who else was involved at the time?"
- Listen. Silence may be helpful in order to let the other person clarify his/her thoughts, perspective and feelings.

Value Perspective

- Hearing and acknowledging a person's perspective is important in understanding and building a foundation upon which to create next steps.
- Empathy is particularly helpful in facilitating understanding when you don't share the same perspective or reaction.
- The key notion is that the other person's perspective is as valid and as worthy as your own.

Evolve an Action Plan together

- Ask for the other person's input, ideas and suggestions first before offering your own ideas.
- Develop an action plan that's SMART. (See page 201)
- Follow up to ensure that you're moving in a positive direction.
- Evaluate results to "close the loop" and ensure a permanent solution.

Prepare for the Discussion

- It's important to think about your approach when providing constructive criticism. Adjust your thinking and language to ensure that the person doesn't feel attacked.
- Think about the topic as an issue to be solved, as opposed to being critical toward someone for something they did wrong.
- Be prepared to listen to the response.

Avoid Blame		Try this
"You really gave me a hard time this morning."	vs.	"I'm confused about what happened this morning at our meeting. Could you please offer some clarification."
"You're always late."	vs.	"I'd like to talk about start times for our day."

Timing

The timing of your constructive criticism should be as close to the event as possible; however, make sure that you can keep your emotions out of the conversation and that the other person will not be upset by the conversation. The objective is to find a positive solution. If you're upset or angry, those emotions may well get in the way of mutual understanding for you and for the other person.

If, during the discussion, you find your own emotions mounting and getting in the way of a productive exchange, stop the conversation as gracefully as you can. There's no point in trying to force yourself into collaboration when you're in an intensely emotional state. You're not able to reason as fully and as creatively as you can when you're in a calmer state. Reschedule the discussion for a time that's more acceptable to you and the other person.

Location

Privacy is key. You want to ensure that other people can't overhear the discussion, as it's potentially personal and sensitive. Find a location that's quiet and where you won't be interrupted. Ensure that you don't feel rushed.

Body Language

A significant amount of your message is conveyed by your body language. You should be seated, with your arms uncrossed, facing the person, and preferably not across a desk. Maintain good eye contact. Try and relax and see this as an opportunity to move forward in your understanding of this person and the situation.

Work Toward Understanding

It takes time, patience and self-discipline to listen and truly hear what someone is saying. Part of your work will be in quieting your internal voice or debating what the speaker is saying. Try to focus on understanding and using empathy by repeating back the message, particularly when you don't agree with the person. The goal is to completely understand each other.

Examples of empathy and testing your understanding:

- "Sounds like you're really angry with our company and with me."
- "I hear that you're disappointed with the path we're on and that you feel we're headed in the wrong direction."
- "So what you're saying is that the schedule won't meet our production needs and you're fearful that we'll fall behind?"

The Value of a Good Action Plan

There are several important elements of a good action plan which are summarized in the acronym SMART.

S	–	**Specific**
M	–	**Measurable**
A	–	**Accountable**
R	–	**Realistic**
T	–	**Time Bound**

Specific ...   Focus on one item/issue at a time.

Measurable ...   Be able to evaluate whether the action was taken or not and the value of the final outcome.

Accountable ...   One person is responsible for the action.

Realistic ...   An achievable action that will impact the final outcome.

Time Bound ...   Assign a realistic timeline.

Hot Buttons – Words to try to avoid

But ...	negates what you said previously
Always ...	talk about one issue at a time
Never ...	same as "always"
However ...	same as "but"
Should ...	judgmental – you're imposing your beliefs

Instead, finish the sentence and start a new one or substitute "and."

"You did a great job of formatting the document. It's consistent and the spelling is perfect. What I'd like to do is talk about punctuation and a couple of principles that might be helpful."

"The meeting was all right and I want to talk about how to make it even better next time."

Honesty and Tact

Reality Bites

It appears that quite a few of us were taught that speaking up and telling our truth was a punishable offence. It was labeled "contradicting, talking back, lying" and generally perceived as being disrespectful. No wonder it's hard for so many of us to speak up and believe that our perspective has merit and that we're part of the solution.

Being honest doesn't mean saying whatever comes into your mind. Being tactful means thinking carefully about what you're saying, why you want to say it, and how you phrase it.

Questions to ask yourself before speaking to someone:

1. Is this important information for this person?
2. Is it just my opinion?
3. Will it affect our working together or his/her ability to do the job?
4. How will this help the other person?

When you're invited to proceed, consider these steps:

1. Position the information in a positive way.
2. Ensure that your comments are about a behavior, not the person.
3. Don't blame, attack or put down the person.
4. Engage the person in the discussion.

Instead of....	Try this
You're a poor leader.	Would you like to hear my thoughts on what would help increase morale?
Your office is always a mess.	I find it a challenge to locate files in your office.
I don't like your style.	Let's talk about how we face challenges at work.
Your notes make no sense to me.	Help me understand how you organized your notes from our meetings.

Conclusion of Finding Solutions

Providing constructive criticism or developmental feedback, is tricky territory. It's a practiced skill, and like many aspects of communication, worth the effort. It provides a valuable learning opportunity that can improve the workplace or a relationship.

LISTEN – ACKNOWLEDGE – ASK

"Every person in this life has something to teach me – and as soon as I accept that, I open myself to truly listening."
~&~
Unknown

INTRODUCTION

To be understood is a powerful and significant human need. The ability to listen, truly hear and let the speaker know that he or she has been understood, is one of the most important communication skills that you can acquire. Misunderstood people feel frustrated, disappointed and discouraged. It's difficult to learn how to listen effectively; however, the benefits are numerous. Using the structure: Listen – Acknowledge – Ask, this section explores the fine art of solution focused conversation.

From the Redmond Journal

A manager in a pharmaceutical company was upset that one of her employees had suddenly quit his job. The manager had made the employee aware of his poor performance by citing everything that he was doing wrong and by letting him know that others thought he was doing a poor job also. Not once during the conversation was the employee allowed to explain his performance, nor was he asked if he required support, additional training or more feedback to help him do his job better. When the employee tried to explain, the manager dismissed his words as "bunk." The next day, the employee quit.

Over the Water Cooler

"I really don't like having to talk to her. Actually no one ever really talks; we just listen. She's never silent."

"He prides himself on being a good listener, but he just fights me every step of the way. He challenges my ideas, tells me not to trust my own judgment and puts down my perspective. It isn't worth trying any more."

"As soon as I start talking about my perspective, she tells me what she thinks and feel. It feels like we're both transmitting into the dark and not understanding each other at all."

"I'm really not interested in listening to you. I've heard it all before and I have my own problems."

Listening Mastery

Reality Bites

Tests have shown that individuals are about 25% effective in listening (Huseman, Hahiff & Hatfield, 1976). In other words, we listen to and understand only about a fourth of what is being communicated. A person listens at a rate of 500 words a minute, and a speaker speaks at a rate of 125-250 words per minute; therefore, it's easy for the listener to get sidetracked – lots of time to think of other things. Listening is a skill that requires focus and discipline.

Listening is the magic in problem solving.
We learn so much when we're silent.

THE THREE STEPS

You can master the listening skill with practice. There are three elements:

1. Listen

Reality Bites

It's so easy to talk to him – everyone says so. He turns off his cell phone, closes the door, forwards his telephone and sits facing you. He just quietly and thoughtfully listens. What a fantastic leader.

Minimize distractions and be available to focus on the other person. Practice Dignity (Strategy Four – Engaging with Dignity) at all times.

Listen to hear intent. Clear your mind of your internal chatter and simply pay attention to the other person. Work hard to hear the whole message, and try to understand the feelings that are being conveyed through words, body language, expression and tone of voice. One of the most powerful things that you can say is, "Tell me more about that."

Wait to offer your perspective until you're sure that you've understood what the person is truly trying to convey.

2. Acknowledge

 Reality Bites I was talking and he was sitting there in silence looking at me, but I have no idea if he heard a word that I said. When I finished talking he starting talking about something else entirely. Do you think he heard me?

Encourage the person's message by nodding or using gentle body language indicators and words to demonstrate that you're paying attention.

Clarify the message with open-ended questions. More information will be provided if you ask an open-ended question as opposed to a closed question, typically answered with a "yes" or "no" response.

Open-ended questioning:

What do you think worked well in our meeting today?

Closed questioning:

Did you think our meeting today was effective?

If someone wants to share exciting news, show interest and understanding through recognition. Recognition may sound like, "You've come so far with that project. It's a great accomplishment." Only say this, the same as any statement, if you sincerely mean it.

If the person is emotional during the discussion, it may be appropriate to respond empathically, saying, "So what you're saying is that the client caught you off guard and you weren't sure how to respond," or "You sound delighted that the meeting ended on such a high note." Hearing the emotion identified assures the speaker that they've been understood. If you're wrong, it's likely you'll quickly be corrected and that's fine. Accepting correction is a healthy part of the communication process.

3. Ask

 After I told him what was going on he said, "OK, here's what you should do," and proceeded to tell me how to solve the problem. I wanted to talk it through and get some ideas, not be told how to fix it. I know he meant well, but this wasn't the support that I was looking for.

Whenever possible, during a problem solving conversation, ask for a solution to the issue. We're often too quick to tell people what we think they should do, when the action, or next steps, actually belong to them. Hesitate to offer advice until the other person has made an attempt to try to solve the problem by him/herself. Listening to others' ideas is an opportunity for great creativity.

Listen - Acknowledge - Ask

Listen	**Acknowledge**	**Ask**
✔ Listen closely to the complete message. ✔ Shut down the chatter of your thoughts and simply try to understand what the person is saying on all levels.	✔ Encourage the speaker through eye contact, body language and gentle comments. ✔ Reflect back what you've heard. ✔ Provide recognition (if appropriate). ✔ Name the emotion (if appropriate).	✔ Seek solutions or next steps. ✔ Provide examples from your experience, not your advice.

Empathic Listening

Consider the perspective of the other person before, during and after a conversation. Understand that everyone has a perspective and that being right doesn't mean that someone else is wrong. Your point of view is right most significantly for you.

Keep an open mind regarding the motives, thoughts and feelings of the other person. You never know why someone is reacting a certain way, until you ask. Listen to the answer. Work to understand. Don't interrupt, debate, challenge, deny or mock the perspective of another person.

Empathizing with someone doesn't mean that you always have to agree. It means that you hear and understand another's perspective. If you work hard to understand how someone else sees a situation, and he or she can do the same with you, you'll make great strides in creating a mutual understanding of the situation in question.

Empathy does not mean that we encourage "complaining."

There's a risk in empathizing with the same person repeatedly regarding the same problem. One needs to move forward and correct the situation, not just talk about it. If you find yourself in this situation, you might say, "Mary, you've talked to me several times about how Paul treats you indifferently. Does Paul know how you feel? If so, what progress have you made so that he'll treat you differently in the future?"

Developing good listening skills takes commitment, diligence, and a sense of humor as you work at applying them. However, over time, you'll find that the hard work pays off. The benefits to your relationships with colleagues and the fact that people trust you to treat them with dignity and fairness, will make your own job much easier, easing your stress level and increasing your chance for success.

Conclusion of Listen – Acknowledge – Ask

These may appear to be three simple steps, but they may not be quite as easy as you think. Listening is a skill that requires determination and discipline. Keeping the spotlight on the person and acknowledging him/her is also challenging, as you often want to jump in and offer your own point of view. Asking instead of telling reaps powerful benefits. The individual has solved and now owns the issue.

Summary of Strategy Four ...
Respect Others

Engaging with Dignity

Key Thoughts
- ○ Every person in the workplace deserves to be treated with dignity.
- ○ Silence is one of the most significant communication skills.

Putting it into Practice
- ○ Practice the 7 steps of Engaging with Dignity.
- ○ Allow more "silence" in your conversations.

Compassion

Key Thoughts
- ○ Judging the person, instead of the behavior, is a destructive force.
- ○ Gossip can sour a workplace.

Putting it into Practice
- ○ Develop the skill of identifying behavior – what the person says and does, doesn't say or do.
- ○ Identify different ways of stopping the spread of gossip.

Focusing on Strengths

Key Thoughts
- Recognizing your colleague's strengths is one of the best contributions you can make to the workplace.
- Providing CREDIT© with good information and timeliness can produce powerful results.

Putting it into Practice
- Look for opportunities to give CREDIT© to colleagues and your leader.
- Evaluate the reaction, short term and long term, of your efforts.

Finding Solutions

Key Thoughts
- One of the most difficult workplace challenges is confronting problem situations.
- SOLVE© is a structure that can guide you through tough conversations.

Putting it into Practice
- Decide on one problem that you'd like to resolve. Identify the behavior attached to the problem.
- Work through a SOLVE© discussion with the person. Evaluate your results, short term and longer term.

Listen – Acknowledge – Ask

Key Thoughts
- Listening is a challenging skill as you can listen more quickly than a person can speak.
- You communicate more profoundly when you keep the spotlight on the speaker by listening, acknowledging and asking, as opposed to entering too quickly into a joint dialogue.

Putting it into Practice

○ Promote others to speak by not interrupting, asking "what else can you tell me" and gentle encouragers like nodding and maintaining good eye contact.

○ Keep the spotlight on people by acknowledging what they're saying and by using empathy when there's emotion in the discussion.

○ Ask open-ended questions to solicit more information and self-discovery.

Moving from Strategy Four to Strategy Five

In *Strategy Four – Respect Others*, you've learned a lot about effective communication. You now understand that it's definitely a two-way process. The concepts of how to communicate with dignity, compassion, optimism and tact, using good listening techniques and SOLVE© to trouble shoot, will help you immensely not only in the workplace, but in every aspect of your life. In *Strategy Five – Harness Conflict*, you'll investigate the good and the bad of conflict and how to harness conflict to increase collaboration and ultimately benefit the workplace.

Water Cooler conversations you'll hear as a result of applying Strategy Four – Respect Others

"I've always felt well treated, even when we had to deal with mistakes and setbacks. It was never personal. We always focused on the issue and what could be improved."

"We spend less time talking and more time trying to truly understand what the other person is saying. It was hard work at first, but has saved us time and money in the long run."

"We now avoid accusations. We focus on how to improve."

"We're expected to give and receive positive feedback to everyone, including leaders and customers. As long as it's concrete and honest, people like to hear it."

"Problem solving is a way of life around here. We confront problems squarely, quickly and with focus. We keep tension and frustration to a minimum this way."

Rules of Engagement for Communicating at Work

STRATEGY FIVE
Harness Conflict

THE GOOD, THE BAD AND THE UGLY

"After all this is over, all that will really have mattered is how we treated each other."

_&._

Unknown

INTRODUCTION

In addition to supporting ourselves, we choose to go to work for many other reasons. Many of us want to enjoy a rewarding career, accomplish a significant piece of work, become part of a productive team, or benefit from the rewards of building a network of colleagues, customers and suppliers. Regardless of the reason, we tend to have high hopes and a positive attitude when we first join an organization. Unfortunately, however, our dreams and hopes are often dashed because of negative office tension, relationship conflicts and an overall sense of dissatisfaction with the organization. While creative tension can have a positive impact on the workplace, negative tension can often deteriorate into conflict and impact the workplace in significant and destructive ways.

From the Redmond Journal

I was somewhat horrified to learn that the CEO of an international organization referred to the marketing department as the "morons" – the Marketing Morons. It wasn't surprising when, one by one, they all left the organization. I followed the career of one person from that department, and I'm thrilled to report that she's thriving in a completely different line of work. Her self-esteem has been restored, she loves what she does, and she's left "that toxic place" far behind her. She learned the meaning of "next" in searching for career satisfaction.

Over the Water Cooler

"Everyone is fighting with everyone.
Who needs it?"

"A good fight clears the air."

"He treats me disrespectfully and that's why I'm quitting."

"I don't say anything to rock the boat. I just slow down my work to get even."

"I just couldn't stand working with him."

The Confines of Conflict
Positive Conflict

"Conflict is the lifeblood of vibrant, progressive, stimulating organizations. It sparks creativity, stimulates innovation and encourages personal improvement."
– Wanous & Youtz, 1986; Pascale, 1990

Different perspectives, work styles, thought patterns and personalities can light a spark that fuels innovation, creativity and progress. The challenge for organizations and leaders is to leverage those differences in a positive, profitable way. Potential sources of conflict include competing agendas, differing points of view, varying solutions, and individual approaches and personalities.

Differences, when managed properly, create an opportunity for in depth learning and creative problem solving. Fear of conflict can cause the Abilene Paradox – a term that refers to a group who agrees to a solution that contradicts its better judgement.

Remaining silent, in spite of heading in the wrong direction doesn't help an organization. In fact, it can let a company slide into difficulty.

Organizations are wise to solicit honest feedback from all key decision-makers. While this process may temporarily lead to conflict, the group will hopefully reach consensus regarding the resolution.

Negative Conflict

Discontent among employees, low morale, or a drop in productivity can be the result of negative conflict.

Stages of Negative Conflict

Differences, if poorly handled, can deteriorate in the following manner:

Dissatisfaction in the form of:
- avoiding others who don't share your perspective
- cliques
- sarcasm
- put downs
- withdrawal from discussion, and
- arguments

Disruption in the form of:
- work disruption
- tardiness
- absenteeism, and
- missed commitments

Sabotage in the form of:
- deliberate, inaccurate forecasting
- deliberate spending over budget
- dropping an important project, and
- withholding essential information

Violence in the form of:
- threats of physical harm
- abuse (verbal, emotional or physical)
- fighting
- destruction of property (cars, lockers), and
- bullying

Conflict Culprits

There are four key areas of conflict: Information Gaps, Style Differences, Goal Differences and Belief Differences.

What Conflict Looks Like ...

Information Gap
   Cause
   - team members with different information, and
   - messages received differently than intended

   Behavior
   - information used as power, preventing some from being able to do an effective job, and
   - misunderstandings that lead to erroneous assumptions

Style Differences
   Cause
   - personality differences,
   - varying range of skills, experience, understanding of business, competencies, and
   - differing work methods

   Behavior
   - differing views on most things in life – work, home, treatment of others,
   - action based on intuition vs. data, and
   - reactive vs. proactive

Goal Differences
   Cause
   - unclear objectives,
   - standards that aren't modeled,
   - changing priorities,
   - hidden agendas, and
   - inequitable resources

Behavior
- team dynamics become strained,
- unprofessional behavior becomes the norm when standards are unclear,
- self- serving behavior to carry out hidden agendas, and
- resentment of resource-rich departments

Belief Differences
Cause
- principles,
- rights,
- responsibilities, and
- values

Behavior
- falsifying information, dishonesty, misrepresentation, manipulation,
- shirking responsibilities,
- self-serving attitude, and
- inconsistent treatment of others depending on position

Symptoms of Conflict

Positive tension can lead to creative conclusions such as unique solutions, intriguing perspectives, feedback that's constructive, misunderstandings that are clarified, and humor that's used effectively.

Negative tension can lead to destructive conclusions such as aggressive competition, arguments, personal conflict, put-down humor, sarcasm, avoidance of problem solving discussions, absenteeism, turn-over and stress related illness.

Whose Conflict Is It?

The people directly involved in the conflict, own it. When there are two people involved in a conflict, the hope is that those two people solve it. If neither has the skills to manage the conflict, then it becomes the responsibility of the leader to try to manage the situation.

Stephen Covey's description of the *Circle of Influence* and the *Circle of Concern* elegantly explain the notion of ownership.

You've probably had concerns when it comes to differences in the workplace – your relationship with your boss, your peers, conflict on the team, other people's relationships within the organization. This is called your Circle of Concern.

As you evaluate your Circle of Concern, it's obvious that you have control over some issues and not over others. Example, you can't control whether two people work well together. Only they can do so. Your focus needs to be on how you spend your own energy and the issues within your own Circle of Influence.

Reactive behavior focuses on the Circle of Concern, which includes flaws in other people, relationships between other people and issues with the company. This focus results in blame, accusations and feelings of victimization. This negative effort causes your Circle of Influence to shrink, as your energy becomes inappropriately distributed.

Proactive behavior focuses your efforts in the Circle of Influence, where you can directly make change. When you focus your time and energy on correcting problems over which you have control, you actually increase your Circle of Influence.

The belief in dealing with differences is that they're most powerfully dealt with by the people who have direct influence over them.

Conclusion of The Good, The Bad and The Ugly

Just as you've experienced positive stress and negative stress in your life, so too, you've probably experienced positive conflict and negative conflict in your workplace. It's a fact of life. Not everyone is going to agree on everything or get along with everyone, everywhere, all the time. So, it's up to you to decide how you're going to manage the conflict in your life. Remember, that differences don't necessarily cause conflict. They can be used as powerful learning tools, heightening your awareness of a different perspective, or creating the springboard for learning a new skill.

YOU HAVE THE POWER

"The rung of a ladder was never meant to rest upon, but only to hold a man's foot long enough to enable him to put the other somewhat higher."

Thomas Huxley

INTRODUCTION

The ability to manage conflict requires both art and science. While it's ideal to try to find a solution that appeases all those in a conflict situation, it's not always possible.

The Thomas-Kilman's Conflict Model clearly develops a process for identifying five strategies for dealing with conflict and effectively suggests corresponding behaviors.

From the Redmond Journal

"I thought that compromise was the only way to deal with conflict. It's made a huge difference for me to understand that it's only one of several options. I'm particularly glad to know that there are times when compromise isn't even a possibility!"

Over the Water Cooler

"She's gutless. She won't have a good fight and clear the air."

"He's a pushover. Just tell him that you can't do it, and he'll do your work for you."

"I'm afraid to stand up for myself. People will be angry at me if they know I see it differently."

"I'm a 'take no prisoners' kind of guy. It works. People stay out of my way."

"Just figure out how to split the difference. I don't want to talk about it. I just want to get going on the work."

Conflict Management Strategies

The Thomas-Kilman Conflict Mode Model

The following model outlines the five modes of behavior and the varying levels of assertiveness and cooperation for each of the modes.

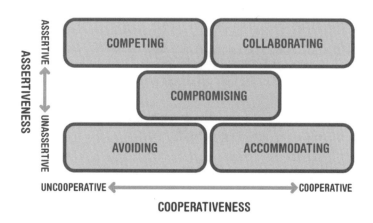

Appropriate and Inappropriate Use of the Five Conflict Handling Modes of Behavior

COMPETING which is Assertive and Uncooperative
Appropriate when:
- standing up for your own rights
- defining a position that you believe is accurate/ important when immediate action is necessary

Inappropriate when:
- digging in your heels just to win

ACCOMMODATING which is Unassertive and Cooperative

Appropriate when:
- another person is in a state of crisis
- there's a better position than your own
- it's not a significant enough issue to disrupt/disturb equilibrium

Inappropriate when:
- giving in just to avoid conflict
- backing down because the other person is more aggressive than you

AVOID which is Uncooperative and Unassertive

Appropriate when:
- the issue is trivial or of insignificant importance
- others can solve the conflict more effectively
- requiring more time to cool down, gather information outside your Circle of Influence

Inappropriate when:
- avoiding conflict because of aggressive stance of other party

COMPROMISE which is Intermediate in Assertiveness and Cooperativeness

Appropriate when:
- dealing with a moderately important issue
- two opponents are negotiating to satisfy their own concerns
- trying to quickly solve an issue
- all else fails

Inappropriate when:
- you're pushed to find a quick solution

COLLABORATE which is Assertive and Cooperative

Appropriate when:
- needing to satisfy both parties
- working through significant issues to find a sustainable solution

Inappropriate when:
- the other party doesn't want to commit the time/effort to develop a solution

Application Strategies for the Four Causes of Conflict

Thomas-Kilman's strategies for resolving conflict are now applied to the four causes of conflict: Information Gaps, Style Differences, Goal Differences and Belief Differences.

Information Gap

Cause
- not everyone on a team has the same information
- a message is received differently than intended

Behavior
- information is often used as power, preventing some from being able to do an effective job
- a misunderstanding can lead to erroneous assumptions

Suggested Solution:	**Collaborate** *Review the information available, go to the source, compare information.* **Compete** *Ask for the information you need.*

Style Differences

Cause
- personality differences
- varying range of skills, experience, understanding of business, competencies
- differing work methods

Behavior
- differing views on most things in life – work, home, treatment of others
- action based on intuition vs. data
- reactive vs. proactive

Suggested Solution:	**Compromise** *Explain your preferences.* **Collaborate/Accommodate** *Work together to assist those with less experience, less developed competencies.* *Work together to include varying perspectives.*

Goal Differences

Cause
- unclear objectives
- standards that aren't modeled
- changing priorities
- hidden agendas
- inequitable resources

Behavior
- team dynamics become strained
- unprofessional behavior becomes the norm when standards are unclear
- self-serving behavior to carry out hidden agendas
- resentment of resource-rich departments

Suggested Solution:	**Compete** *Challenge those who are self-serving.* *Defend your need to establish priorities and to build common objectives.* **Compromise** *Establish consensus regarding standards.* **Collaborate** *Ensure all information regarding resources is available and share what's available equitably.*

Belief Differences

Cause
- principles
- rights
- responsibilities
- values

Behavior
- falsifying information, dishonesty, misrepresentation, manipulation
- shirking responsibilities
- self-serving attitude
- inconsistent treatment of others depending on position

Suggested Solution:	**Compete** *Seek and speak the truth.* *Challenge the actions of manipulators and inconsistent treatment or behaviors.* *Live by your values and set of rules in building relationships.* *Hold others accountable for their responsibilities.* **Avoid** *When you perceive the relationship as destructive and unproductive*

Conclusion You Have the Power

The more skilled you are at dealing with conflict, the more likely you'll be to realize a positive outcome. Effectively managing conflict calls upon all the personal attributes and skills that you've learned so far: character, self-care, dignity, compassion, tact, collaboration and conversation. With practice, you can alleviate many potentially explosive situations, or in the event that conflict does arise, (which it inevitably will) you now have some practical tools to help you develop workable solutions.

BULLIES AT WORK

"You don't know what power you have until you make choices in a hard time."

Lord Dragnys

INTRODUCTION

The issue of bullies at work has been prominently discussed in recent years. Bullying, which is defined as generalized workplace abuse, is four times more common than sexual harassment. (J. Richman, American Journal of Public Health, 1999). Bullying can slide under the radar due to the deviousness and machinations of its inherent behavior. Violence is rare, but bullying is estimated to affect one in five workers in the U.S. workforce. The cost of bullies in our workplaces is difficult to estimate, but we do know that stress related illness has staggering consequences both to individuals and to organizations.

From the Redmond Journal

From back alleys to boardrooms, I'm sorry
to report that the bully is alive and well
in today's society and workplace. But take
heart, even bullies have their weak spots.
And when you know what they are,
you're well equipped to counteract their
noxious behaviors.

Over the Water Cooler

"He comments on everything that I do or say."

"There are two sets of rules – one for her and one for everyone else."

"Nothing is ever good enough."

"Even trying to go the extra mile gets turned into a negative."

"Everything that I do or say is used against me."

Brazen Bullies

Reality Bites

I'm afraid of my staff. There have been so many times when they'll team up and go to Human Resources or to my boss to complain about something I've said or done. Then I'm forced to defend myself. When I go back to our department, after being hauled in to HR, I feel like everyone is waiting for my reaction. I feel undermined and paralyzed, unable to do a proper job. I wouldn't dare discipline anyone. It isn't worth the backlash.

According to The Campaign Against Workplace Bullying Survey, the top ten bullying tactics are:

1. blaming others for errors
2. making unreasonable job demands
3. criticizing ability
4. noncompliance with rules
5. threatening job loss
6. insulting sarcasm
7. discounting/denying accomplishments
8. excluding or "icing out"
9. yelling, screaming
10. stealing credit

The Bully Mindset

Reality Bites

It took all the courage I could muster to go to my boss and tell her that Karen was making my life at work miserable. I detest conflict, but her non-stop put-downs, refusal to share information and degrading comments were causing me sleepless nights and trouble focusing at work. My supervisor took the issue to Human Resources and had a meeting with the four of us. I felt like I was on trial. No wonder no one ever complained publicly about her. I went on sick leave because of the unbearable stress of having to work with Karen, and I'm dreading going back to work.

Bullies search for people who will allow themselves to be treated poorly because in the mind of a bully, the target is powerless.

Nice By Nature

Dr. Gregory S. Berns, a psychiatrist and author, found that among the women in his practice, most of them chose "mutualism" over "me-ism" – collaboration over conflict. He found that the longer subjects engaged in a cooperative strategy, the more strongly the blood flowed to the pathways of pleasure. "It's reassuring," Berns said, "in some ways we're wired to cooperate with each other." No wonder that it's often difficult to confront inappropriate behavior. Even our wiring seduces us to cooperate.

Back Off, Bully!

When you're confronted by bullying behavior:

- compete – don't appeal to the bully's sense of fair play, chances are it doesn't exist,
- be firm and clear about your expectations,
- be factual and honest about the subject of the bully's taunts,
- be true to yourself, firmly maintaining your boundaries, and
- keep your emotions removed from the situation – bullies want you to be hurt, offended, or even scared.

Language to use with bullies sounds like:

- "You interrupted me five times. Let me finish my thoughts without interruption."
- "Stop touching me."
- "Move further away from me."
- "You took the report off my desk and that's not acceptable."
- "Don't make assumptions about my choices. Ask me."
- "Could you explain your comment to the team."

Take Control

You don't have to be rendered helpless or label yourself the victim just because you're the target of bullying. Your best defense is to take control of the situation – to regain your power.

In order to do this, you can:

- get advice from a professional on how to effectively confront and reply to the bully,
- confront the bully and reply appropriately, documenting every incident including time, location, and a description of the bully's behavior,

- tell the bully that you're taking the situation to the next higher level in the organization if the problem continues, and do so,
- involve the Human Resource Department, and/or the Employee Assistance Counselor in the situation – document these actions,
- arrange for witnesses to the bullying behavior – document and sign the information, and/or
- seek legal advice.

Reality Bites

"Our senior team meetings were dreadfully painful and lasted well into the night. The new president pushed, pinpointed, degraded, mocked and belittled us without fail. Two of our colleagues took early retirement and he brought in people from his previous company. When he asked why I resigned, I told the truth. I was beyond being humiliated at this point in my life. He shrugged his shoulders and we never exchanged another word. I understand that those meetings are still as ugly as ever. The people remaining are reluctant to quit in this job market – too many people depend on their jobs. One person has gone on long term disability due to stress, I doubt anyone will ever know what really goes on." This type of description is unfortunately, very common.

Conclusion of Bullies at Work

The Drama Triangle (Strategy Three) is a structure that can help you understand the inappropriate behaviors of bullies and can encourage you to defend your position. You don't have to succumb to the negative influence of bullies. That's exactly what they want. Plan your defense carefully, asking for help if necessary, and take back your control with confidence and courage.

FORGIVE, FORGET, FORGE ON

"The weak can never forgive. Forgiveness is the attribute of the strong."

Mahatma Gandhi

INTRODUCTION

We seem to live in an angry world. Whether we're enraged at the driver in front of us, frustrated with the obnoxious parent in the hockey arena, or incensed with a colleague, it seems that tempers flare easily these days. And while you might have to face the fact that you're surrounded by potentially volatile situations, you don't have to succumb to them.

How you deal with the person who cuts you off on the highway, or grabs your parking spot at the grocery store, is totally up to you. You have a choice. You can get angry, or you can let it go. Anger can have negative and long term emotional and health consequences. Dealing with it is a skill and needs to be practiced, just like every other skill already covered in this book. When you learn to release your anger, work through your feelings, and deal with the pain you've been caused, you are poised to move forward.

From the Redmond Journal

Did you know that it takes more energy to hold a grudge, than it does to deal with and let go of your anger? Your energy can be much better used by forgiving others their shortcomings, imperfections and errors in judgement. I certainly hope that others forgive me for my imperfect humanity, for my sake as well as theirs.

Over the Water Cooler

"There's no way that I'll ever forgive her, she doesn't deserve it!"

"If I let it go, he'll just start up all over again. All my progress will evaporate!"

"I have to be angry. That's the only way I can keep up my guard."

"She has never, to this day, acknowledged that she did anything wrong."

"He couldn't care less how I feel. He laughs when I say how hurt I am."

Let It Go

Anger is an emotion, which sometimes can evoke out-of-control feelings and irrational thinking. Anger can immobilize you or move you to action to protect others or yourself. Anger also elicits resentment – a feeling that festers inside your head, usually magnifying the original incident which made you angry in the first place. Resentment builds negative energy. It also puts your health and well-being at risk and diminishes the potential for pleasure that you could receive from life with your children, your partner, your colleagues, and yes, even the other hockey parents!

When the other person has the courage and wisdom to acknowledge the pain you are experiencing, whether intended or not, it is relatively easy to forgive them and move to a new level of trust in your relationship. To forgive doesn't mean you have to condone or tolerate inappropriate behavior. Your boundaries can remain firmly in place, protecting your beliefs, dignity and self-respect.

When the person chooses not to acknowledge your perspective, it is more difficult, but still possible to forgive. Forgiveness is a gift that you give to yourself. It's a promise to yourself that you won't let someone else's actions or words cause you unhappiness or pain. Forgiveness is a sign of strength, maturity and intelligence.

Reality Bites

Ted and Eric worked side by side, in a machine shop, for over 20 years. Many years ago there was an argument between them and they stopped speaking to each other. So he would never forget, Ted wrote a reminder of the incident on a piece of paper and kept it in his work clothes. Whenever Eric tried to make amends, Ted would take out the ragged piece of paper, read it and shun Eric's overture for reconciliation. The dome of silence was preserved.

Take Action

In an ideal world people wouldn't treat others disrespectfully, either deliberately or by accident. But we don't live in an ideal world, so here are some suggestions to help you deal with anger causing situations:

1. Use SOLVE©.
2. Be honest with your feelings and ensure that those who have elicited your anger understand the reasons why.
3. Explore options to ensure that the occurrence isn't repeated in the future.
4. Choose to let your negative feelings dissipate.
5. Consult your Employee Assistance Program or pursue other counseling opportunities if your angry feelings persist.

Forge On

In Dr. Robert Enright's powerful book *Forgiveness is a Choice*, he offers four phases which identify the stages of anger and then he explores the methods for dealing with it.

Phase 1 – Uncovering your Anger
- How have you avoided dealing with anger?
- Have you faced your anger?
- Are you afraid to expose your shame or guilt?
- Has your anger affected your health?
- Have you been obsessed about the injury or the offender?
- Do you compare your situation with that of the offender?
- Has the injury caused a permanent change in your life?
- Has the injury changed your worldview?

Phase 2 – Deciding to Forgive
- Decide that what you've been doing hasn't worked.
- Decide to be willing to begin the forgiveness process.
- Decide to forgive.

Phase 3 – Working on Forgiveness
- Work towards understanding.
- Work toward compassion.
- Accept the pain.
- Give the offender a gift – material or moral (such as deciding to show compassion).

Phase 4 – Discovery and Release from Emotional Prison
- Discover the meaning of suffering.
- Discover your need for forgiveness.
- Discover that you're not alone.
- Discover the purpose of your life.
- Discover the freedom of forgiveness.

This process is designed to build confidence in the way we manage acrimonious situations, by understanding why we feel and react the way we do, and by taking steps to alleviate the negative impact that anger can cause.

Conclusion of Forgive, Forget, Forge On
Your decision to forgive another person is the starting point for this process. Forgiveness is a relief for you, the person who feels wronged. There are physical, emotional and practical benefits to moving on from the situation. Your decision and actions will add to the enjoyment of your work.

Summary of Strategy Five ...
Harness Conflict

The Good, The Bad and The Ugly

Key Thoughts
- ◯ Conflict, well harnessed, can have a positive effect on the organization.
- ◯ The four cause of conflict are Information Gaps, Style Differences, Goal Differences and Belief Differences.

Putting it into Practice
- ◯ Watch for symptoms of conflict in your organization and determine if the stage is Dissatisfaction, Disruption, Sabotage or Violence.
- ◯ When there's conflict examine the following: the cause of the conflict and the owner of the conflict.

You Have the Power

Key Thoughts
- ◯ There are five Conflict Handling Modes in the Thomas-Kilman Model: 1. Compete 2. Avoid 3. Compromise 4. Accommodate and 5. Collaborate.
- ◯ There's a time and place to use all five Modes.

Putting it into Practice
- ◯ Find an example of conflict and determine the cause and the Conflict Handling Mode most appropriate for dealing with it.
- ◯ Apply the Mode and evaluate the outcome.

Bullies at Work

Key Thoughts
- ❍ Bullies can be any person in any role.
- ❍ The common tactics bullies employ are: blaming others for errors, being unreasonable and critical, behaving in a threatening, aggressive manner and undermining others.

Putting it into Practice
- ❍ Identify bullying behavior.
- ❍ Take control of the situation by confronting the person. If the behavior continues, go to leadership for support.

Forgive, Forget and Forge On

Key Thoughts
- ❍ It's to everyone's advantage, especially yours, if you forgive inappropriate behavior.
- ❍ Dr. R. Enright suggests four concrete steps to forgive: Uncover your Anger, Decide to Forgive, Work on Forgiveness and Discovery and Release from Emotional Prison.

Putting it into Practice
- ❍ Identify the person at work whom you need to forgive.
- ❍ Work through the four steps to forgive, forget and forge on.

Water Cooler conversations you'll hear as a result of applying Strategy Five – Harness Conflict

"There's virtually no conflict in our organization. There's creative tension, but it produces great collaborative results."

"People enjoy each other's differences."

"We're really clear about what's our business and what belongs to someone else. Everyone in the organization knows not to get involved in other people's conflicts. We listen, acknowledge, and ask for clarification, but we don't interfere or take sides."

"We don't tolerate abuse. People are encouraged to confront the offender and/or escalate the assistance process if they're feeling put down, intimated or threatened. They inform the other person of the steps they're taking."

"We solve our issues and move on. Everyone knows that holding on to anger and grudges hurts the whole organization."

CONCLUSION OF *RULES OF ENGAGEMENT FOR COMMUNICATING AT WORK*

There are many ways for you to create your own success both at work and in your personal life. It begins with communication, and it's dependent on many other factors that build upon your ability to communicate well. You can't depend on luck for your success. You have to plan a strategy for it, envisioning what your success looks like and then taking action to make it happen. There will be obstacles along the way in the form of those who will challenge your values and ideas, who will create conflict, and who will make you angry. Remember, you can use those obstacles to your advantage – they're the springboard for learning. Stay true to your goals, to your belief in your self-worth, to your model for treating others with respect, and to your commitment to transform your vision into reality, and then revel in your ability to thrive in the workplace and in all areas of your life.

Congratulations! You've now completed the *Five Strategies for Decreasing Conflict and Increasing Collaboration*. The Strategies depend upon each other and no one Strategy is more important than the other. The challenge is to successfully find your balance. Best wishes on your journey.

Leading Your Team

Putting the Five Strategies into Practice
as a Leader

Rules of Engagement for Communicating at Work

LEADING YOUR TEAM – PUTTING THE FIVE STRATEGIES INTO PRACTICE

Strategy One – Clarify the Culture

Communicate your Way to Success
Putting it into Practice as Leader

- ○ Be prepared to answer questions regarding structure, history, systems and programs. Simple, clear information can be as effective as elaborate roll out campaigns. The key is to ensure that your team understands the basic infrastructure of your organization.
- ○ Ensure that every person can articulate the purpose of the organization and how his/her job contributes to the purpose.
- ○ Clarify the values of your department. Ensure that the five or six ways that you want to do business are understood and practiced by all (e.g. tell the truth at all times, treat each other with dignity, consider customers in all decisions, share information openly).
- ○ Clarify your expectations, as specifically as possible, of each position, project and task. Provide feedback on all aspects of performance: what each person is striving to achieve as well as his/her behavior as they work. Articulate any gaps between actual and expected performance. Apply SOLVE©.
- ○ Develop ground rules, as a group, at the commencement of each meeting. Ask the meeting members to help manage adherence to the rules.

Pratfalls and Protocols
Putting it into Practice as Leader

- ○ Learn to spell and pronounce the name of every person on your team.

○ Establish communication with every team member on a regular basis. One-to-One sit down meetings on a consistent rotation will pay huge dividends. Two way exchange of information, feedback and alignment of goals and projects are suggested agenda items.

○ Keep record of your One-to-One meetings, particularly action plans and results.

○ Encourage your team members to track their own performance. They own their job. Results of projects, feedback received, learnings garnered from experience form part of their record keeping and tracking systems.

○ Help your team members find mentors, both internal and external.

Common Courtesy
Putting it into Practice as Leader

○ Hold a meeting with your team and decide on the "common courtesy" acceptable to all. Develop a process for ensuring that courtesy is practiced.

○ Develop, with your team, a protocol for dealing with email, voice mail, cellular telephones and other communication devices.

○ Keep your team up to date on organizational developments. Clear, open communication reduces time spent speculating.

Good Cheer
Putting it into Practice as Leader

○ Encourage laughter and fun at work. It will help the work get done and make the workplace pleasant.

○ Find your own way to introduce humor at difficult moments. Tension is reduced and people feel physically better when they laugh.

○ Ensure that humor is used positively and that no one is suffering negative consequences.

You and Your Team
Putting it into Practice as Leader
○ Demonstrate your ability to collaborate with your team members, your leader, other departments and stakeholders.
○ Encourage people to work together as the end result will be better (for most projects).
○ Ensure that team members clarify messages and information as misunderstandings are very common.
○ Include all potential partners in ensuring your success: customers, suppliers, shareholders as well as all members of the organization.

Strategy Two – Know your Character

You're Wired
Putting it into Practice as Leader
○ Observe your teammates and colleagues on a regular basis to see if anyone is having difficulty keeping control of himself/herself in conversations. Talk to your team about what causes them stress, the physical warning signals when they lose control and their plan for managing themselves in difficult situations.
○ Monitor to see if your team members are adjusting their interactions by observing the reactions of others. Help them to examine and refine their own behavior to support others in a difficult situation.

Knowing Your Intent
Putting it into Practice as Leader
○ Clarify, with your team, their beliefs regarding how they interact with each other.
○ Explore communication rights and responsibilities as a group.

- Help people understand their objective in an interaction by coaching them with the following questions; "what do you hope to achieve?", "what is the best possible outcome of that situation?" and "what would success look like in that circumstance?"

You Say Nature, I say Nurture
Putting it into Practice as Leader
- Evaluate the individual strengths, talents and contributions of each team member.
- Help your team recognize and acknowledge the gifts that each person brings to the team. Ask how to best maximize individual talents.
- Explore personality differences on the team. Develop alternatives to capitalize on the differences.

Self Esteem at Work
Putting it into Practice as Leader
- Recognize the symptoms of low self-esteem. Guide team members towards enhancing their self-esteem based on the communication thoughts.
- Encourage your people to be candid about what they see as appropriate and inappropriate in the workplace.

Strategy Three – Respect Yourself

Workplace Boundaries
Putting it into Practice as Leader
- Discuss boundaries with your team in terms of principles, values, priorities, standards and safety issues.
- Observe your team to understand who tends to be responsible "for" and "to" and in what circumstances. Discuss your findings with the person.

○ Encourage the use of "I" statements by all team members.

○ Clarify your vision of the use of "I" and "we" statements.

Standing Your Ground
Putting it into Practice as Leader

○ Discuss the Transactional Analysis concept of "I'm OK and you're OK" with your team. What does this mean, internally to your team and with the rest of the organization?

○ Ask your team when they feel lured onto the Karpman Drama Triangle? What can they do to get off the Triangle?

○ Does anyone believe that there are real victims within the organization? What is the circumstance and what can be done to support the person?

Feedback: The Ultimate Learning Opportunity
Putting it into Practice as Leader

○ Evaluate how well the individuals on your team receive feedback.

○ Provide feedback to a team member and ask them to practice the W5 for receiving feedback.

○ Provide feedback on how well the person listened. Ask for implementation thoughts resulting from the discussion.

○ Observe your team members receiving feedback from each other. Provide insights regarding any game you see being played to avoid hearing the message.

Strategy Four – Respect Others

Engaging with Dignity
Putting it into Practice as Leader
- ○ Encourage your team to practice Engaging with Dignity.
- ○ Develop an understanding as a team, of how a person should react when they're not treated with dignity.
- ○ Encourage people to interact more carefully and allow more "silence" in their conversations.

Compassion
Putting it into Practice as Leader
- ○ Encourage a focus on judging behavior, not people.
- ○ Discourage gossip in the workplace.
- ○ Encourage people to care about the success of each person on the team.

Focusing on Strengths
Putting it into Practice as Leader
- ○ Provide positive feedback using the CREDIT© model generously. Do so only with planning and concrete information. Document the discussion, providing a copy to the person and keeping a copy for your records.
- ○ Encourage people to provide CREDIT© to each other.
- ○ Ask your team members to provide CREDIT© to you when they believe it's warranted. Express thanks when they do so.

Finding Solutions
Putting it into Practice as Leader
- ○ During your One-to-One discussions with your team members, ask them for examples of problems that they would like to solve with you and other people.

○ Help each person to develop a plan to use the SOLVE© model to deal with the problem. Evaluate the results of the conversation with the person. Ask for learnings and encourage the person to keep on practicing this problem solving technique.

Listen – Acknowledge – Ask
Putting it into Practice as Leader
○ Encourage your team to listen to each other more profoundly and use the Listen – Acknowledge – Ask structure.
○ Evaluate progress after three months in order to evaluate if there are fewer mistakes and better solutions to problems.

Strategy Five – Harness Conflict

The Good, The Bad and The Ugly
Putting it into Practice as Leader
○ Encourage differences as they can lead to greater creativity.
○ Observe any symptoms of negative conflict on your team.
○ Investigate and determine the cause.

You Have The Power
Putting it into Practice as Leader
○ Decide on a plan to manage negative conflict using the Thomas-Kilman Conflict Handling Modes, as appropriate for the situation.
○ Apply the strategy and evaluate the outcome. Adjust and continue as necessary.

Bullies at Work
Putting it into Practice as Leader
○ Discuss the subject of bullies with your team. Ask if anyone feels bullied or if they know of anyone else in the organization who feels that way.

○ Confront the issue as appropriate and follow up to ensure that the problem has been solved.

Forgive, Forget, Forge On
Putting it into Practice as Leader
○ Encourage your team to forgive past problems with you, each other, customers, the leadership or any other individual or group associated with the organization.
○ Support your people as they work through the steps: forgive, forget and forge on.

Troubleshooting

Questions	Find Answers in ...
Is communication really all that important?	
How do I find out what's expected of me?	
What can a mentor do for me?	
What should I say about my organization?	
What to do when you're fed up and close to retirement?	
What's considered common courtesy?	
Is it ok to laugh and enjoy work?	
Why is there so much emphasis on collaboration?	
Why do I struggle to say what I know I should say?	
What does communicating really mean?	
What has my character got to do with communication?	
How do I build trust with others?	
What do I do with a personality conflict?	
Does self-esteem influence how people work together?	
It is challenging working with so many people and so much pressure. How do I keep my balance?	
How do I know if I'm being manipulated?	
How do I work with people I don't like and trust?	
I know I should provide more positive feedback, but I don't know how.	

Strategy	Section
One	Communicate your Way to Success
One	Pratfalls and Protocols
One	Pratfalls and Protocols
One	Pratfalls and Protocols
One	Pratfalls and Protocols
One	Common Courtesy
One	Good Cheer
One	You and Your Team
Two	You're Wired
Two	Knowing your Intent
Two	Knowing Your Intent
Two	Knowing your Intent,
Three	Workplace Boundaries
Four	Focusing on Strengths and Finding Solutions
Two	You say Nature, I say Nurture
Two	Self Esteem at Work
Three	Workplace Boundaries, Standing Your Ground and Feedback: The Ultimate Learning Opportunity
Three	Standing your Ground
Four	Engaging with Dignity
Three	Workplace Boundaries
Four	Finding Solutions
Four	Focusing on Strengths

Questions	Find Answers in ...

I detest conflict. What do I do when things go wrong and I know I should talk to the person?

I know it is important to listen to people, but I'm not sure how to go about it?

We have conflict here but some conflict is good. How do I know the difference?

What's my business and what isn't when other people are in conflict?

I see people bullied – what do I do?

Some people don't deserve to be forgiven – why should I?

What do I do as the leader?

Glossary

Abilene Paradox (page 222)
- A term that refers to a group of people who agree to a solution that contradicts its better judgement.

Accountability (page 232)
- Accepting the consequences for the outcome of a situation for which you're responsible.

Adult-to-Adult Communication (page 140)
- Communication based on the notion that we're each responsible for our own actions. Based on the Life Position, I'm Ok, you're Ok. Interaction that is based on behaviors, thoughts and feelings which are direct responses to the here and now.

Amygdala (page 68)
- Located in the brain's medial temporal lobe, the almond-shaped amygdalae are believed to have strong connections to our mental and emotional reactions.

Amygdala Hijack (pages 70, 71, 72)
- Our brain's emergency control reaction, triggering a fight or flight response. Information can travel directly to the thalamus and then to the amygdala.
- The amygdala can trigger an emotional response before we understand what's happening. We react before we "think."

- It's critical to recognize our emotional reaction and manage our response as appropriate to the actual situation.

Arrogance (page 242)
- Having or revealing an exaggerated sense of one's own importance or abilities.

Authentic Communication (pages 2, 3, 4)
- Being truthful about our intent, thoughts and feelings.

Blame (page 199)
- Assigning responsibility for a problem to an individual.

Bullying (page 242)
- The repeated, malicious verbal mistreatment of a target individual driven by the bully's desire for control.
- Control is typically a mixture of cruel acts of deliberate humiliation or interference and the withholding of resources and support, preventing the target from succeeding at work.
- A bully's actions can damage the target's health and self-esteem, relationships with family and friends, economic livelihood, and/or a combination of all of these.

Character (pages 2, 3, 4, 82)
- Who we are as a person as defined by our intent, IQ, EI, personality and engagement skills.
- Our ability to understand, develop and align these elements results in better communication.

Chronic bullying (page 242)
- Persisting for a long time or constantly reoccurring.

Communication Principles (page 83)
- What we believe to be true.

Communication Values (pages 23, 84)
- How we believe we should behave based on the Principles.

Constructive Criticism, Feedback for Improvement, (page 196)

- The ability to present an issue from your perspective, to include the other person by asking for his/her perspective, to brainstorm a solution and to evolve an action plan.

CREDIT© (page 188)

- A model, structure, template for providing positive feedback.
- Circumstance, context. Recognize, reinforce Exactly what the person Did. Identify The outcome, impact.

Dignity (page 168)

- The minimum level of courtesy we demonstrate in our interactions with others.

Dysfunctional Power (page 242)

- Coercing, shaming, blaming, threatening, scheming and humiliating other people. They may be aggressive and threatening or charming and feign cooperation.

EI – Emotional Intelligence (Communication) **(page 74)**

- Our ability to recognize our own emotions and those of others, and manage our actions and reactions in order to communicate effectively.

Engagement Skills (page 4)

- The words that we use and the interaction skills that we employ to communicate with others.

Emotion (pages 68, 69)

- The state of your body-mind-heart at any given point in time, triggered by memories, thoughts, a situation, a scent, or other stimulation. It registers in your body in different ways – called "feelings."
- The main categories of emotion are anger, sadness, fear, enjoyment, love, surprise, disgust and shame.

Empathic Listening (page 209, 212)

- To listen with the intent to understand – to respond to both the emotion and the message of the speaker.

Empathy (pages 209, 212)

- To understand the view of another person – to be able to put yourself in the other person's situation.

Filters (page 55)

- The beliefs, values and interpretation that influence our perspective and reception of messages.

Freedom (page 232)

- Making the choices that you believe are most appropriate in any given situation.

Functional Power (page 154)

- People who are fair and balanced in their approach. They're team players and work toward a "win-win" outcome.

Healthy Boundaries (page 122)

- The ability to believe in your own judgment and proactively manage your choices and relationships. You choose the level of familiarity and intimacy in your relationships.

Goals (page 121)

- What you intend to achieve within a certain time frame, or situation.
- Priorities, objectives and standards.

Identity (page 122)

- Defines who you are and what you want.

Intent (pages 2, 3, 4, 82)

- What a person is trying to achieve through his/her words and actions.
- Comprised of (1) Beliefs: Principles, Values, Rights and Responsibilities; (2) Goals; Priorities, Objectives, and Standards.

IQ – Intelligence Quotient (pages 2, 3, 4)
- A number representing a person's reasoning abilities as measured by problem-solving tests.

Nature/Nurture debate (pages 94-99)
- Nature means we were born with a predisposition for certain aptitudes. Nurture means that we've been socialized or trained to behave the way that we do.

Personal Power (pages 122, 123)
- What you believe you should do and the action you take.

Personality (page 94)
- The combination of characteristics, qualities, talents and gifts unique to an individual.

Perspective (page 55)
- One way to look at a situation, person or action.

Physiology (page 68)
- The branch of biology that deals with the normal functions of living organisms and their parts.

Politeness (page 37)
- Having or showing behavior that's respectful and considerate of other people.

Position Power (page 20)
- This is the level and scope of authority in your job.

Positive Reinforcement (page 188)
- Encouraging positive behavior by providing specific, concrete feedback (e.g. CREDIT©).

Positive tension (page 222)
- Creative energy that stems from differences effectively presented and managed.

Pratfall (page 127)
- A foolish or humiliating action.

Proactive Behavior (page 132)
- Taking responsibility for one's actions – being aware of one's thoughts, feelings and beliefs and making decisions accordingly.
- Requires a healthy internal value where one can choose to be optimistic regardless of the behaviors of others.

Protocol (page 120)
- The accepted or established code of procedure or behavior in any group, organization or situation.

Reactive Behavior (page 132)
- Responding in reaction to others' behaviors, thoughts and feelings.

Responsibility (page 84)
- Answering for the outcome of a situation.

Rigid Boundaries (page 129)
- Keeping people at a distance.

Rules of Engagement for Communicating at Work
- Appropriate and effective workplace communication
- Character is at the heart of the model and the Five Strategies work in unison to create the end result
- Five Strategies
  1. Clarify the Culture.
  2. Know Your Character.
  3. Respect Yourself.
  4. Respect Others.
  5. Harness Conflict.

Self Care (page 130)
- Respecting and asserting one's own needs and beliefs.

Self-Esteem (page 104)
- Confidence in the ability to think and to cope with the basic challenges of life.

- Confidence in the right to be successful and happy – to assert one's needs, to achieve one's values and to enjoy the fruits of one's efforts. (Nathaniel Branden).

Selfishness (page 142)

- Lacking consideration for others; concerned chiefly with one's own personal profit or pleasure.

SOLVE© (page 196)

- A model, structure, template for a problem solving discussion.
- Specify the Facts of the Situation, Listen to the other side, Value their Perspective and Evolve an Action Plan.

Thomas-Kilman Conflict Mode Indicator (page 232)

1. Accommodating.
2. Collaborating.
3. Competing.
4. Compromising.
5. Avoiding.

Transactional Analysis (page 140)

- Life Positions:
    I'm OK, you're OK.
    I'm not OK and you're OK.
    I'm OK, you're not OK.
    I'm not OK, you're not OK.

Triggers (page 68)

- A person, situation, words, scent or event that causes an emotional reaction related or unrelated to what's actually happening at that moment.

Weak Boundaries (page 129)

- Allowing people to manipulate you.

Reference Page for Models

Glossary

References

Strategy One – Clarify the Culture

Margerison, C. and **A. Kakabadse**, *How American Chief Executives Succeed*, New York: American Management Association, 1984.

Curtis, D.B; Winsor, J.L; and Stephens, D. 1989. National preferences in business and communication education. Communication Education 38:6-15.

The Conference Board of Canada, Organizational Performance Group, October 25, 2002. Prepared for the Secretariat for Managers' Community.

Whetten, David A., Cameron, Kim S. *Developing Management Skills.* New York, Addison-Wesley, 1998.

Wendy's Restaurants. Wendys.com. With permission of **Patrick McCann**, Training Director, Wendy's Restaurants of Canada.

Strategy Two – Know Your Character

Ledoux, Joseph. *The Emotional Brain: The Mysterious Underpinnings of Emotional Life.* New York, Touchstone, 1996.

Goleman, Daniel. *Emotional Intelligence. Why It Can Matter More Than IQ.* New York, Bantam, 1995.

Ledoux, Joseph. *Synaptic Self: How our Brains Become Who We Are.* New York, Viking Press, 2002.

Seligman, Martin E.P., PhD. *Learned Optimism. How to Change Your Mind and Your Life.* New York, Pocket Books, 1998.

Jung, Carl Gustav. *Psychological Types.* Princeton, Princeton University Press, 1976.

Merrill, David W, and **Reid, Roger H.** *Personal Styles and Effective Performance.* New York, CRC Press,1999.

Branden, Nathaniel. *The Six Pillars of Self-Esteem.* New York, Bantam, 1995.

Strategy Three – Respect Yourself

Stewart, Ian and **Joines, Vann.** *TA Today, A New Introduction to Transactional Analysis.* Nottingham, England, Russell Press Ltd.1987.

Covey, Stephen R. *The 7 Habits of Highly Effective People, Powerful Lessons in Personal Change.* New York, Fireside, 1989.

Beattie, Melody. *Codependent No More. How To Stop Controlling Others and Start Caring For Yourself.* Minnesota, Hazelden, 1986.

Cloud, Dr. Henry, Townsend, Dr. John. Boundaries. *When to Say Yes, When to Say No, To Take Control of Your Life.* Michigan, Zondervan, 1992.

Strategy Four – Respect Others

Harris, Thomas A., M.D. *I'm Ok-You're Ok..* New York, Avon Books, 1973.

Kegan, Robert, Lahey, Lisa Laskow. *Seven Languages for Transformation. How The Way We Talk Can Change The Way We Work.* San Francisco, Jossey-Bass, 2001.

Scott, Susan. *Fierce Conversations. Achieving Success at Work and in Life, One Conversation at a Time.* New York, Penguin, 2002.

Weaver, Richard L., II. *Understanding Interpersonal Communication.* Illinois, Scott, Foresman and Company, 1981.

Whetten, David A., Cameron, Kim S. *Developing Management Skills.* New York, Addison-Wesley, 1998.

Strategy Five – Harness Conflict

Namie, Gary, Ph.D., Namie, Ruth, Ph.D. *The Bully at Work*. Illinois, Sourcebooks, Inc., 2000.

The Campaign Against Workplace Bullying – conceived in January 1998 on the Internet (www.bullybusters.org).

Enright, Robert D., Ph.D. *Forgiveness is a Choice. A Step-by-Step Process for Resolving Anger and Restoring Hope*. Washington, DC, APA Life Tools, 2001.

James K. Rilling, David A. Gutman, Thorsten R. Zeh, Giuseppe Pagnoni, Gregory S. Berns, and Clinton D. Kilts. *A Neural Basis for Social Cooperation*. Neuron 2002 35: 395-405.

Kathleen and her seasoned team of facilitators, coaches and program developers work with organizations, large and small. Clients are located in Canada, United States, Europe and the Caribbean.

Books and variety of learning solutions are available on our website. Services are available in English and French.

Please call at 905.478.7982 or visit our website: kathleenredmond.com.

Thank you and best wishes,

Kathleen